MANAGING CHILDREN WITH PROBLEMS

Edited by Ved Varma

CASSELL

This book is dedicated with affection and esteem to
Joan M. Hutton and Robin Higgins.

Cassell
Wellington House   127 West 24th Street
125 Strand   New York
London WC2R 0BB   NY 10011

First published 1996

British Library Cataloguing-in-Publication Data
A catalogue record for this book is available from the British
Library.

ISBN 0–304–33330–1 (hardback)
     0–304–33331–X (paperback)

Typeset by York House Typographic Limited
Printed and bound in Great Britain by Redwood Books,
Trowbridge, Wiltshire

CONTENTS

Contents

CONTRIBUTORS

K. Eia Asen, Consultant Child Marlborough Family Service; Consultant Psycho-therapist, Maudsley Hospital London

Philip Barker, Professor, Departments of Psychiatry and Paediatrics, University of Calgary, Canada; Staff Psychiatrist, Alberta Children's Hospital, Calgary

Maurice Chazan, Emeritus Professor of Education, University of Wales, Swansea; Fellow of the British Psychological Society.

Francis Dale, Principal Child, Adolescent and Adult Psychotherapist, South Devon

Ali EL-Hadi, Consultant Adolescent Psychiatrist, Brookside Young People's Unit, Redbridge; Honorary Senior Lecturer at St Bartholomew's Medical College, London

Steve Fuller, Consultant Clinical Psychologist, Liverpool

David Jones, Senior Lecturer in Psychology, Birkbeck College, University of London

W. Gordon Lawrence, Visiting Professor of Organisation Behaviour, School of Management, Cranfield University; Director, IMAGO East-West, London

Marietta Marcus, Consultant Psychodynamic Psychotherapist, Richmond-Upon-Thames, London

Hitesh Raval, Clinical Psychologist, Gayton Child and Family Service, Harrow; Senior Lecturer in Psychology, University of East London

Jean Sambrooks, Consultant Clinical Psychologist, Liverpool

Colin J. Smith, Senior Lecturer in Education, University of Birmingham

Ved P. Varma, formerly educational psychologist at the Institute of Education, University of London, Tavistock Clinic, London and London Boroughs of Richmond-Upon-Thames and Brent

Harinder Mohan Verma, Consultant Psychiatrist, Brynhyfryd Hospital, Forden Powys, Wales

FOREWORD

In recent years there has been an expanding literature on the problems of children and adolescents, on which the present book focuses. This is an encouraging development, particularly as many of the publications about children with problems aim, in the way that this book does, at increasing the knowledge and skills of parents, teachers and others in regular contact with children. Such an aim is very worthwhile, since, whatever specialist expertise is required, parents and teachers have to be closely involved in any programme of intervention, and indeed in most cases take on the major role. This is well illustrated in the chapter by K. Eia Asen, who discusses ways of helping families, and Colin Smith, on the management of children in school. The role of the family in the causation and treatment of children with problems has long been recognized, but, as David Jones points out, many of the difficulties reported today are in some way associated with education and life at school.

The contributors to this book discuss the problems of children and adolescents from a variety of angles. In the collection of papers four main principles are paramount, which those concerned with problem children would do well to bear in mind. First, it is essential that a detailed and thorough assessment be carried out so that an appropriate plan of action can be worked out, as the chapters by Philip Barker, and by Jean Sambrooks and Steve Fuller, testify. The assessment needs to be delineated in precise terms and, as Hitesh Raval and others emphasize, should be considered in the light of an understanding of the social, community, school and family contexts, the child's physical condition and cognitive level, and other relevant factors. Second, in the words of Asen, problems are partly social constructions: a child's behaviour may be perceived very differently by different individuals and agencies. It is, therefore, imperative to take account of the problem from the point of view of the parents and school as well as of the child. It is also vital to recognize that what is seen as normal or acceptable behaviour in one culture may be viewed differently in another culture. As EL-Hadi puts it, services to children and their families should be culturally sensitive.

Third, the assessment and treatment of problems in childhood and adolescence require a multi-faceted approach and usually the involvement of a number of disciplines, as highlighted by Barker. Disabilities rarely come singly and a child's problems can seldom be attributed to one specific cause. Harinder Verma's contribution, for example, shows that children with special needs arising from learning disabilities are especially vulnerable to behaviour difficulties, not least because their families are often under great strain. Fourth, this book stresses that the key to successful management is good communication: between professionals and clients, within a clinical team or a school staff, and among professionals based in different parts of the support system. EL-Hadi refers also to the need to attempt to correct distorted patterns of communication within the family.

Although, as Jones asserts, prevention is likely to be far more effective in the long term than attempts at the short-term management of established problems, there is currently a growing demand from parents, teachers and others for prompt help in coping with children's problems. This book clearly demonstrates that a wide range of therapies and management strategies is available, including individual and group therapy, family therapy, behaviour modification and medication.

A pleasing feature of this volume is that the contributors acknowledge, even when advocating a particular approach in which they have special expertise (such as Francis Dale in discussing psychodynamic approaches), that some problems may require other kinds of help. This book, which is yet another valuable addition to the many publications edited by Ved Varma, deserves a wide readership.

Maurice Chazan

PREFACE

The management of children with problems worries us all. There is a great need to know more about them, about how they feel, think and behave.

This book is a modest attempt to consider what can be done in this respect. The contributors include psychiatrists, psychologists, psychotherapists, and educationalists. All write from a background of first-hand experience and distinguished work with difficult children and adolescents. I hope and pray therefore that this book will prove valuable to students and practitioners in education, psychology, psychiatry, psychotherapy, counselling and social work.

Without the able and perceptive help of Naomi Roth, my Cassell editor, this book would not have been possible. Thanks to her I have much enjoyed editing it.

Ved P. Varma

Joan M. Hutten: An Appreciation

by W. Gordon Lawrence

In the 1990s we are experiencing the deconstruction (to use a polite word) of the health system and the education service in Britain because of the Conservative government's policy of reducing the funding of all social services. To be sure, we can talk of the original conception of the health service, which Aneurin Bevan launched with such passionate single-mindedness on behalf of the Labour government, as now being a lost good object. The reality is, however, not to be gain-said. In Britain we are experiencing an undeniable loss – the death of an ambitious, unprecedented social ideal – and it is against this background that the authors of the chapters in this book have to carry out their professional work. They are not easy conditions, but each writer shows his or her commitment to developing good practice even in demanding situations which are exacerbated by ever scarcer resources.

The life and work of Joan Hutten with children with problems demonstrates that this current government's short-term policy is questionable, if not downright flawed. It can safely be predicted that the policy will in the future result in Britain having an adult population with a higher incidence of delinquency and mental health problems. These will be of a magnitude which has never been experienced in our history previously. The costs will be borne by later governments and, more importantly, will result in psychic suffering for large numbers of citizens, impairing their political and spiritual potentialities as adult human beings. Joan Hutten, in short, has always worked on the principle that prevention is better than cure and that early intervention is more cost-effective than having to repair damage later in time when the initial difficulty will have become that much more entrenched and far less tractable.

Children with problems can be understood to be children who are experiencing, for whatever reason, an arrest, or hiatus, in their normal development. This results in their experiencing feelings and being in emotional states which are difficult to bear, if not intolerable. Consequently they have no way of understanding their own aberrant behaviour. If, however, they can be worked with at this time in their lives and given space in which to examine their problems so as to find reasons for their feelings and behaviour, their chances of recovery are enhanced. They are, thus, better able to sustain their own maturation and development. Joan Hutten has always represented the conviction and value of intervening early in the cycle of the generations for the benefit of both the individual and society.

The key to Joan Hutten's work with children with problems is that she has centred her approach on working with the parents of such children. This is based on her hypothesis that it is remedial work with parents of problem children which is critical. Her work has been designed to enable the parents of children with problems to discover their own inner resources for taking on the responsibility and authority for parenting. This has meant developing with parents ways by which they can manage the conditions in the family for their problem children to find the desire and ability to reach out for maturity. Part of this work has been to identify with parents what difficulties they themselves experienced in their own family of origin and which hampered their own growth. This is because their own past difficulties will be being mirrored and acted-out with their own children. This approach identifies and addresses the multi-generational factors in child-rearing. Discerning the effect of past parental experiences on current life in the family enables the parents to understand what conscious and unconscious climate they are generating for their children and what may be impeding their potential for growth to maturity. This work of creating a mental space for the parents to reflect on how they can help their children's development is an admixture of a therapeutic alliance and the provision of a modelling of 'good enough' parenting. This work of helping adults to find their skills as parents she sees as a necessary element in working with minors who by definition cannot be totally responsible for themselves.

Long before it became fashionable Joan Hutten was conceptualizing and working with the family as a system, embedded in a sequence of personal biographies and history, and situated in an environment which is both demanding and bewildering and not always a facilitating one. She came to this view on the basis of her observation of children in families and by knowing the problems of children through experience rather than through knowing *about* them.

This intellectual stance of knowing through experience was helped by her own psychoanalysis. She readily volunteers that through personal analysis her own ideas began to change and this was pivotal in her going on to further develop those ideas. But she had always believed that one discovers insight through thinking with other people and developing ever better practice. The other side of this is her respect for children. She believes it is a privilege to work with children because they see the world with questioning eyes. Children, however, are socialized into seeing reality from the adult's perspective which, sadly, can often destroy their own creative apperceptions which may come up with much better formulations of what reality is and could be.

Throughout her work one is aware that she is always in dialogue with both children and parents and tries to create the conditions for parents and children also to be in dialogue, because this two-way process offers the opportunity for mutual mental growth of both child and adult.

One puzzles about one's colleagues. What made them what they are?

Joan Hutten started her working life in the Royal Liverpool Children's Hospital in 1939, the year that the Second World War broke out. At Brighthelmston School in

Birkdale, Southport, in Lancashire she had gained the Oxford Higher School Certificate in the same year. She stayed in nursing for ten years, becoming a State Registered Nurse and passing the examination to be a midwife. Her nursing skills took her to the Copenhagen State Hospital (1947–48) and into a spell of private nursing. Most women would have continued their lives in this fashion staying with a career that had a solid foundation in practice and qualifications.

But Joan Hutten was not cast in such a mould. At the age of twenty-seven she went to Liverpool University to take the Social Science Certificate which she gained in 1951. In the same year she went to work for three months in France at a children's hospital, a children's village for war orphans and a holiday camp for maladjusted children. Early in her work life Joan Hutten was seeking out experiences that were to lay the foundations for her later professional life.

From Liverpool she moved on to the London School of Economics where she took the Certificate in Mental Health in 1952. Because she was such a good student Kay McDougall sought her out subsequently to become a lecturer in Mental Health at LSE in 1956. In the meanwhile Joan Hutten had worked in the Hertfordshire Child Guidance Service and the St George's Hospital Child Guidance Clinic. After her appointment at LSE she worked in the Great Ormond Street Hospital Child Guidance Clinic. Taking time out for full-time child rearing (her son was born in 1961 and her daughter in 1964) she did, however, in 1963 and 1967 act as a locum lecturer in Mental Health at LSE.

In 1970 she joined the Tavistock Clinic in the Department for Children and Parents, becoming Principal Social Worker five years later. This role she held till retirement in 1987. She tells me that what impressed her about work at the Tavistock was that the policy was that there should be no teaching or research without clinical work and that everyone took his or her share of management and administration. She was comfortable with this policy because throughout her life she has combined clinical work with teaching, writing and administration and has never lost touch with practice.

No account of her work should miss that in 1971 she was asked by her departmental executive committee at the Tavistock to establish an interdisciplinary programme for brief focal intervention which would develop criteria for the selection of appropriate referrals and monitor outcomes. This programme ran for six years and the results were published in her book *Short Term Contracts in Social Work*, published by Routledge and Kegan Paul in 1977. This work informed subsequent part-time unidisciplinary courses which Joan Hutten ran for social work practitioners burdened with casework and immersed in work systems which carry horrendous responsibility without adequate support. The time spent by practitioners on a course, even of only one and a half hours per week, provides them with a reflective space out of real time, so to speak. Her method of working with practitioners is a combination of consultancy and teaching.

The other innovation for which Joan Hutten is to be remembered is the course called 'Child Care, Practice, Policy and Research'. In 1983 she was stimulated by an article by Michael Rustin and Carol Satyamurti of the then Polytechnic, now University, of East London about enabling experienced social workers to do case-based, qualitative research for a higher degree while remaining in post. She recruited three interested colleagues and together they designed a course involving a day-and-a-half release per week during term time for two years. In the second of these years students submitted research proposals to the sponsoring university.

This course proved to be the prototype for several other similarly linked training/ higher degree programmes in the Tavistock Clinic as a whole. Although the student numbers were small (with an alternate-year intake) and although it took time for participants to complete their theses after the taught course, there is now for the first time a cohort of practice-based research M Phils; several of these degrees have been converted to D Phils. Joan Hutten is a supervisor for the D Phil degree.

Privately, Joan Hutten sees this course as a memorial to her son David who was killed on his bicycle in 1975 by a motorist who drove on without stopping. David Hutten was 14 years of age at the time.

What are the qualities that make Joan Hutten the teacher-mentor that she is? She has taught at the London School of Economics and the Tavistock Clinic as well as in a variety of other contexts. There seems to be no doubt that her students have appreciated her enormously and gone on to achieve distinction in their chosen fields.

One reason why Joan Hutten is a good teacher is that she always allows people to think things out for themselves. She has done this by her own commitment to private, reflective thinking which, I believe, allows her to give space for others to do the same. One feature of her teaching is her capacity to be silent. Disconcerting for some students of a dependent nature, to be sure; but liberating for others because they feel that they have been given mental space to be available for thinking as opposed to learning up received opinions.

The ability to entertain silence, I suspect, is linked to an ability to allow for 'reverie' in the teaching situation. I am thinking of Winnicott's (1971) ideas on the mother-baby relationship, but only as a metaphor. Between teacher and taught, to use conventional terms, we can think of a 'third space': a cultural space between them into which ideas can be put and played with creatively. But for that space to be invoked or convened, so to speak, the one in the role of the teacher has to have a built-in capacity for reverie – which cannot be taught and is only acquired by experience.

Another reason is that Joan Hutten works at participating in the events and happenings that make for experience. She takes part in experiences and partakes of them whether these be of a professional nature or just of going on holiday to somewhere new, like a cruise on the Nile or a visit to Petra. Her consequent reflection enables her to develop her working hypotheses, her interpretations, if you will, which will always be of a fresh nature. Theory comes after experience, not before, with Joan Hutten. And my hunch is that this ability to experience her experiences – no matter how irksome – makes her a different kind of teacher because her students can internalize, perhaps quite unconsciously, this mental disposition in relation to their own experiences. It is this commitment that allows for the development of ideas and thinking which are based in realities and not in theory, which is one of the reasons why, later in life, her students too can go on to develop their ideas and write about them.

As I work with Joan Hutten I am always struck by her ability to add to thought. She never takes away, subtracts, diminishes in the way of people who introduced their remarks with: 'But . . . ' At the same time, if there is shaky thinking she is the first to question it, often in a quizzical way, and if she feels the thinking is tawdry or slipshod she will point that out quite firmly.

On rare occasions she sometimes seems impatient. In my experience this is because she feels that the person in question really ought to be striving to know better for him- or herself and so is not realizing his or her potential. She is also of a practical turn of mind. There is a time for reflection and a time for action; a time for silence, a time for voicing one's beliefs; a time for tolerance and a time for saying that this course of action will lead to disaster.

The work of Joan Hutten has been recognized over the years in the invitations she has received to conduct seminars in Clermont-Ferrand, Rome, Perugia, Oslo, Athens, Toronto and at Cornell University. She has also done a large amount of consultancy to staffs of children's homes, members of religious orders, hospices and schools. She has regularly taken experiential learning groups for psychotherapy and counselling trainees, psychiatrists, nurses, psychologists and music therapists. And a few years ago she was among the pioneers in taking groups of people to help them understand the critical issues relating to retirement. She, of course, continues to do this work of taking experiential learning groups as well as consulting and supervising.

In parallel to her practice, Joan Hutten has continued over the years to enlarge her own educational experience. She became a full member of the Group-Analytic Society in London, at the invitation of its founder Dr Foulkes, and has undergone psycho-analysis at the Institute of Psycho-Analysis.

I came to know Joan Hutten through group relations education in the Bion-Tavistock tradition. As I listened to her contributions I knew that here was someone with whom I would be glad to work. I have been fortunate in that she has made herself available to work with me in working conferences in France, England and Ireland over a number of years. In this she has been a solid anchor and has trained another generation of people in understanding unconscious social processes in groups, institutions and society. I am always enriched by her presence on the staff of such working conferences because she always provides me with a good role model of how one just has to try to stick with understanding one's experience, no matter how demanding, and not take refuge in intellectualism.

These life experiences and qualities have made Joan Hutten the teacher that she is; someone who is always prepared for dialogue and of sufficient generosity of mind and spirit to provide the conditions for others to take authority to make themselves available for experiencing and thinking.

It is fitting that this book should celebrate her life of working with children with problems, for each of the contributors has written a lively and thoughtful chapter that brings before the public, and – one hopes – before our political masters, the necessity to take care today of our children who are to be the citizens of tomorrow.

REFERENCE

Winnicott, D.W. (1971) *Playing and Reality*. London: Tavistock Publications.

Robin Higgins: An Appreciation

by Marietta Marcus

Robin Higgins, a consultant child psychiatrist, has combined a career in medicine with a lifelong interest in music and the arts.

As a psychiatrist, he worked at the Hospital for Sick Children, Great Ormond Street, at University College Hospital, at Willesden Child Guidance Clinic, and at the Tavistock Institute of Human Relations. During the twenty years before he took early retirement from the NHS in 1988, his appointments included Richmond and Twickenham Child and Family Consultation Centres, the Medical Centre at Goldsmiths College (where he provided a psychiatric service to students and staff), and various special schools for children with emotional and physical problems.

On the musical side, while studying medicine at Cambridge, he was a choral scholar at King's College. He later continued his theoretical musical training by completing the B Mus at London (University College). After retirement, he joined the staff at the Laban Centre for Movement and Dance, where, on the dance movement therapy course, he was engaged with case presentation and research projects. The outcome of this work was two books published by Jessica Kingsley: *Approaches to Case-Study* in 1993 and *Approaches to Research* in 1996.

I once asked him what he enjoyed about his work. It was, he said, 'the ability of the young and those open to learning, to elicit the shadow ... in themselves, their families, and the world at large. They have a knack of spotting the hidden elements in situations, and of suggesting ways to redress imbalances.'

He suggested that in their reveries, children have many subtle ways of handing back to the adult, in more digestible form, the problems they were set. In this sense he sees children, and the Child in us all, as creative and resilient rebels. Perhaps what he meant was that life could be one great therapeutic playground – given a good therapist, flexibility and lateral thinking.

CHAPTER 1

Children with Problems: Past, Present and Future

David Jones

It has often been suggested that to ignore history is to risk repeating its mistakes. Perhaps this warning is nowhere more apt than in the upbringing of children. We pride ourselves on living in an age of enlightenment; successive governments have reported ever-increasing expenditure on education; and yet there are worries about juvenile delinquency and job prospects for school-leavers. We have witnessed a series of extensive reforms of the school system, but worries about the level and quality of provision for children with special educational needs have not gone away. Never before has the world community given such prominence to children's rights in the hope of creating a better future. In 1989 the United Nations General Assembly approved the Convention on the Rights of the Child (Document A/RES/44/25). This wide-reaching statement sets standards for the rights of children in family law, social welfare, education and health. In the United Kingdom the Children Act England and Wales 1989 provided a comprehensive legislative structure for childcare practice and the safeguard of children's rights (White, Carr and Lowe, 1990). The justification for action by the state is defined in terms of actual or likely harm to the child. Harm is taken as including physical, sexual or emotional abuse. The Children Act emphasizes that the best interests of the child should be the guiding principle for all decision-taking on the care of children by social services departments and the courts. We recently lived through 1994, the International Year of the Child. It is appropriate, therefore, to ask why there are still so many concerns about problems in children.

History has already made many of us aware that children represent the future for any society. Politicians of all parties acknowledge that expenditure on childcare and education is justified as investment in the future. Sadly there are differences in judgements about what make good investments. Many in society remain reluctant to make more than token contributions through taxes for the care of other people's children. Some politicians appear willing to be complacent about increasing class sizes in state schools. Others feel it is fair game to join the act of criticizing the teachers whenever standards fluctuate. We run a great risk of allowing social divisiveness to escalate, with the children from a large section of society leaving school with feelings of anger and resentment over lost opportunities. Such feelings of alienation

1

become significantly greater when school-leavers have few satisfying career prospects. Disturbingly there are children leaving school who have grown up in homes where their parents have never worked.

It would be alarmist to suggest that our civilization is at risk, but many fear that the lessons of history have already been ignored for too long. Political correctness and the legal system have properly wrestled with the need to create a climate of racial equality, but there is a greater danger that the inequalities of social class have been ignored for far too long. There are countless examples in history of tensions and hatred arising from perceived differences in social structures (Jones and Barrett, 1993).

Much has been written about cycles of disadvantage. It is far from easy to interpret research findings when parenting breakdown appears to be associated with such a large cluster of social and environmental disadvantages as the sociological literature and the press have identified. Evidence of problems in two or more members of a family and then also in the next generation does not in itself confirm causal environmental influences. The early work of Rutter and Madge (1976) suggested that some patterns of inter-generational links could be identified. For example, men convicted of physical violence towards children tended themselves to come from large families and to have been exposed to physical abuse and lack of continuity of care. The National Child Development Study reported by Davie, Butler and Goldstein (1972) pointed to such factors as young motherhood, large family size, single-parent homes, illegitimacy and a history of reception into care as being associated with educational and behavioural problems in children, as well as with physical abnormalities.

Quinton and Rutter (1988) focused on admission of children into care as an index of parenting difficulties, while recognizing that such breakdown may arise from a variety of factors. They provide a sophisticated interpretation of the interactions between family functioning characteristics and parenting capacities on the one hand and continuity or change in social adversity on the other. From their findings in both a retrospective and a prospective study, there was evidence at a statistical level that mothers who had been in care themselves were more likely than those in comparison groups to be associated with ratings of poor parenting skills. Nevertheless Quinton and Rutter emphasize that these associations were far from inevitable and that two-thirds of the mothers in their prospective study had not experienced parenting breakdown in their interactions with their own children. Indeed, about a quarter of the ex-care mothers were rated as showing good current parenting. Marriage to a non-deviant or supportive spouse was associated with a level of quality of parenting by the ex-care mothers similar to the comparison group. In addition, attention is drawn to the need to identify those families in which parenting breakdown is associated with psychiatric disturbance in the parents and the complex ways that such disturbances become linked in the creation of adverse environments for the children.

The title of the current book is almost a cry of despair in so far as it focuses on the management of children's problems. We should also ask why there are so many children with problems. There is a need to reflect on the causality of the problems. There are no simple answers and we must avoid the mistake of adopting a simple model of linear causality. As in the example already given of the research on cycles of disadvantage, there is a need to be aware of complex interactions between background factors. A brief reflection on the perceived roles of children in families and in society in past generations may bring some of these interactions into a sharper perspective.

REFLECTIONS ON THE HISTORY OF CHILDHOOD

The systematic study of child development is a relatively recent branch of scientific inquiry. Recording of detailed observation of children began with the diary descriptions of the development of individual children little more than a century ago. Prior to that it seems that many children received little more than a few years of care and protection during the dependent stages of infancy and early childhood. Relatively few children received any education or training. The majority, particularly those from socially disadvantaged backgrounds, were treated as miniature adults long before they reached physical maturity. Surviving artwork shows that in past centuries children were often dressed in the same way as adults. Many were treated quite harshly and the laws of society provided them with little protection against abuse in the home and in the workplace. Those detected of committing crimes or showing disrespect for authority were likely to be punished almost as severely as adults. Yet there is evidence that as far back as the pre-Christian period children, at least those from privileged families, were indulged to the extent that they had a range of toys. Sommerville (1982) refers to reports from ancient Mesopotamia and Sumeria on the pressures placed by families on sons to submit to the demands of education. Both the Greek and Roman civilizations appear to have used slaves to assist in the education of boys of the ruling classes. Yet there is disturbing evidence that many early societies practised infanticide. Little is documented on the treatment of girls in these societies. The detailed survey of the evolution of childhood by DeMause (1974) suggests that the further back in history one goes, the lower the level of childcare and the greater the abuse of children. Yet from what we now know about the processes of attachment we can speculate that throughout history many children have also been cherished.

It is a reasonably hypothesis that in previous centuries many young children were the victims of the struggle for survival faced by their families and that with the industrial revolution there was a disturbing move to systematic economic exploitation of children. Many boys worked long hours in factories and mines, others worked as messengers and street vendors. Girls from the working classes often went into residential domestic service, providing the immeasurable support for the way of life of the middle classes until the 1920s. Even as recently as the start of the First World War childhood ended abruptly for many children on their twelfth birthday when they reached the current school-leaving age. In the 1920s there were still 'hiring fairs' in some districts for the new school leavers (Humphries, Mack and Perks 1988). There are still adults alive today able to testify to the deprivations imposed on children in the early years of the twentieth century.

A slightly more charitable interpretation of the treatment of children at work arises from the view that by and large adults did not know how else to keep children off the streets. Hugh Cunningham (1991) in his book *The Children of the Poor* provides a vivid account of the tribulations of children at work and also highlights the apparent fear in many adults of allowing groups of children to roam the streets uncontrolled. In the days before compulsory schooling there seems to have been a genuine concern that unsupervised children would get into mischief or crime. It must be remembered that the proportion of children in society was higher than it is today, and that large numbers were orphaned and in some form of institutionalized or charitable care.

Unfortunately, before the advent of the welfare state, children were not infrequently an economic drain on their families until such time as they were able to make a contribution by sharing in food production, or in the running of the home or by earning money. It was not uncommon for children to be passed into the care of relatives or neighbours for several years, or even permanently, so that there was one less to feed in the family home. In extreme cases children with learning difficulties were sometimes abandoned. Children who rebelled were likely to have been given firm discipline. For many years the prevailing philosophical view was that children were essentially blank slates and that their characters could be moulded by firm handling.

A different perspective on the treatment of children is given in the reviews of the history of the treatment of mental disorders by Parry-Jones (1992, 1995) which suggest that prior to the mid-nineteenth century insanity in children and adolescents was either ignored or treated in the same way as in adults. From then onwards medical records indicate a changed approach to the care of juvenile mental health problems. In 1867, Henry Maudsley referred to seven forms of childhood insanity. Medical authorities often cited severe shocks and frightening experiences as precipitating factors in cases of severe emotional disturbances in children. Centuries ago, concerns over bed-wetting were recorded. Some reports even offer the opinion that too much indulgence was to blame for some cases of disturbed behaviour.

In the first half of the twentieth century new theories emerged in psychiatry and psychology which recognized the importance of childhood for later life in a variety of ways. Both psychoanalytic theory and behaviourism recognized the importance of early experiences for later development. The scene was set for the emergence of multidisciplinary teams to staff the child guidance clinics and attend to the problem behaviours of children in a modern age.

Awareness of the harsh conditions imposed on many children at work in the nineteenth century resulted in a series of protective legislative measures. A recognition of the importance of education to prepare children for adult life followed, perhaps motivated in part by the increasing requirements for greater skill in the workforce. The gradual acknowledgement of the rights of children from working-class backgrounds and the subsequent changes in childcare practices served to highlight the importance of childhood experiences within the home. Providing children with educational toys and games was already a feature of affluent homes in the eighteenth century. For example, John Spilsbury is reported to have devised jigsaw versions of maps to help teach children geography as far back as the early 1760s (Vandivert and Vandivert, 1974). By the Edwardian era attempts to stimulate the development of children were more commonplace. Meccano sets invented by Frank Hornby in 1901 quickly became popular as toys to give to boys training in mechanical and practical skills.

It is all the more surprising, therefore, to find that recognition of the value of providing continuity of care across the years of childhood did not become the subject of formal scientific debate until after the publication of Bowlby's report to the World Health Organisation in 1951 on the potential consequences of maternal deprivation (Bowlby, 1951). From the point of view of the public the childcare experts remained divided on what was to be considered as good practice in parenting. There is a disturbing sense that we have so many difficulties in the management of problems in children because the long-overdue move to recognize children's rights somehow leap-frogged the willingness and motivation of adults to accept the responsibilities of parenthood.

PRESENT PROBLEMS: SOME NEGATIVE VIEWS

Despite the major advances in the welfare state and the parallel growth in knowledge about many of the processes involved in child development, there are still many adults who feel terrorized and victimized by children. Unfortunately these feelings are not confined to just those who live in big cities. News reports draw attention to the multiple acts of vandalism committed by children and adolescents, and it seems that the elderly are not infrequently the victims. Media reports suggest that the involvement of young adolescents in offences involving the taking away and vandalizing of motor vehicles has increased considerably in recent years. The police sometimes complain that they lack effective powers to detain and deter child offenders. Sadly, improving children's rights has not solved the problems of juvenile delinquency. Modern society has given children leisure time and mobility and a minority of them do present a challenge to law and order. This is not an argument for reducing children's rights, but it does highlight that the legal system and workers in the caring professions must make even greater efforts to understand the aetiology of conduct disorder and delinquency. Prevention is far more effective than attempts at management of established problems.

Distinctions between the terms 'conduct disorder' and 'delinquency' are not always consistently made in the literature. Conduct disorder is used as a category in psychiatric classification systems and sometimes as a description of antisocial behaviours. Delinquency in a juvenile refers to behaviour which would have been labelled as criminal if committed by an adult. At the present time in the United Kingdom, children younger than 10 years of age are deemed to be below the age of criminal responsibility and would not normally be categorized as juvenile delinquents. Adult victims of child offenders find this distinction hard to accept.

Precise figures on the frequency of acts of antisocial behaviour are difficult to obtain. Surveys using self-report measures tend to find that a majority of adolescents admit having committed at least one minor delinquent act which went undetected. Reported offences are higher for boys than for girls, and incidence levels are highest for boys from lower socio-economic backgrounds. For the most part the boys with a single recorded offence are not greatly different on assessment variables and background from those with no criminal record, and most authorities would want to resist labelling them as maladjusted. It seems that persistent offenders tend to start their delinquent activity at a young age. The success level of currently-practised intervention techniques for delinquency is not good. Cognitive behavioural methods used in training self-restraint techniques in children and adolescents with conduct disorders and in those who have frequent temper outbursts have a moderate degree of success.

Many adults are also fearful because they perceive present-day adolescence as synonymous with a frightening drug culture. There is a lot of misunderstanding about substance misuse. Adults misusing alcohol and tobacco make unfortunate role models and are cited by adolescents to justify their own claim to freedom of choice. Experimentation with drugs and solvents is at such a high level in our society that it is almost unrealistic to think of it as a disorder. The majority of adolescents who take drugs perceive themselves as taking acceptable risks. Often they are able to quote others they know who have used drugs without apparent ill-effects. Unlike delinquency the problem of substance misuse occurs in adolescents from most socioeconomic backgrounds. Estimates suggest that up to one in five may have experimented with cannabis in some form by the end of their teenage years. Use of heroin and cocaine seems to be at a much lower level in this age group, although currently there is speculation that the level might be increasing. The vast majority of those who experiment with drugs will not continue to take them regularly. Secondary problems arise when adolescents turn to crime to finance their drug-taking. A further disturbing trend is the recent dramatic rise in the taking of hallucinogens, often in connection with attendance at rave parties or other musical events.

The negative image of adolescents roaming the streets and posing a threat to social order is further compounded by the rise in homelessness in this age group. Sadly even today there are many cities in the world where street children exist in sizeable numbers as a result of poverty, neglect, political unrest or bereavement. They are perceived as a threat to law and order or a public nuisance and are sometimes subjected to harsh treatment. In our own society homelessness has become a way of life for a minority of adolescents. Some are the victims of broken homes and earlier abuse. Prevention is necessarily better than belated attempts to contain or hide away a disturbing subculture. The root causes of homeless merit more detailed investigation.

Even though Bowlby's claims about the likely consequences of maternal deprivation perhaps exceeded the evidence he was able to cite, the subsequent controversy served to stimulate the enormous growth of research into the importance of parenting and child care. Bowlby's own later theorizing on the significance of attachment in personality development has provided a further landmark in the history of child development research (Bowlby, 1969). Attachment theory provides one of the few points of meaningful interaction between psychiatry, psychoanalytic theory and psychology. It is possible to see how social disadvantage can often create an environment in which continuity of care is difficult to maintain, but for many children poverty does not deprive them of a warm and supportive caring relationship. The same theory helps explain how children from seemingly affluent backgrounds are likely to experience feelings of vulnerability and rejection when they encounter family conflicts.

EDUCATION AND PROBLEMS IN CHILDREN TODAY

It is ironical that so many of the problems reported in children today are in some way associated with education and life at school. The provision of schooling for all children was partly seen as a way of liberating them from unreasonable demands at work or in the home. An additional hope was that schooling would help to compensate for differences in background. Sadly, for a minority of children school is a place where they fail and they perceive themselves as failing. Others find the pressures excessive even though they have the cognitive abilities to cope with the academic demands. A few examples of the categories of children who experience and/or create problems at school will serve to illustrate the challenge to teachers.

Children with learning difficulties

Prior to the Education Act 1970 (Handicapped Children) the responsibility for the education of children who were considered retarded was placed on health authorities. In the period that followed, special schools for children who were 'moderately educationally subnormal' and 'severely educationally subnormal' provided segregated teaching. The term 'learning difficulties' came into widespread use following the Warnock Report (DES 1978) with the intention to minimize the stigma attached to children needing special educational provision. The Education Act (1981) made it possible, at least in theory, for the majority of children with special educational needs – including those with learning difficulties – to be educated within mainstream schools with appropriate extra teaching or the provision of non-teaching support staff.

Education theory and political correctness have become intertwined. Problems arise not least because there are not unlimited financial resources for special needs provision. In an education system which has been through a period of rapid change and embraced adherence to a National Curriculum, regular monitoring of pupil performance, and the publication of league tables for examination results, it is not surprising that increasing numbers of schools have become less than enthusiastic about accommodating children with special educational needs. There may well be advantages for many schools in creating an environment which both parents and children accept as competitive. There are few advantages for children with problems who all too quickly come to perceive themselves as unwanted and suffer the loss of self-esteem which it had been hoped integration would eliminate.

Children with specific learning difficulties

This category includes specific problems in reading, numberwork, or some other area of performance, in children who are otherwise functioning at average ability levels or higher. The term 'dyslexia' refers to specific reading difficulties. Before the expectation of universal literacy, reading failure would have passed unnoticed. The causes and exact characteristics of dyslexia remain the subject of debate (Snowling, 1987). Boys appear to be affected more often than girls. Children who experience difficulties in language acquisition in the pre-school years often have a struggle with the complexities of grapheme-phoneme correspondence when they start to learn to read. Not all cases of reading difficulty meet the criteria for a diagnosis of dyslexia. Failure in reading for whatever reason is often associated with secondary problems such as acting-out behaviour or negative attitudes towards schoolwork generally.

Attention-Deficit Hyperactivity Disorder (ADHD)

This disorder is listed in the American Psychiatric Association Diagnostic and Statistical Manual of Mental Disorders (DSM-IV) (1994). It is characterized by inattentiveness and overactivity/impulsiveness. There have been several variations in the naming of this condition and precise definition over the years. In the International Classification of Diseases (ICD-10) (World Health Organization, 1992) there is reference to a category called hyperkinetic disorder characterized by marked in-attentiveness in a variety of situations. Both classification systems emphasize that the condition is pervasive, usually being manifest in school, home and clinical settings. Problems have usually been apparent since early in childhood. Containing ADHD children in the classroom is far from easy. It is even more difficult to gain their sustained attention in learning situations. Parents are often desperate by the time they seek help. With the move away from child-centred education towards more formal teaching practices in the early years of schooling, children with ADHD come into conflict with the system often before the age of seven years. Child and Family Clinics are facing increasing numbers of referrals for children with ADHD under threat of exclusion from school. Debate continues over the efficacy of ritalin (methyl-phenidate) and other forms of stimulant medication in the management of ADHD.

Children with conduct disorders

From the point of view of mainstream schools, children with conduct disorders, acting-out behaviour and aggressive tendencies are in some ways the greatest chal-lenge. Not only are such children at risk for underachieving in examinations, but also their disruptive tendencies are a threat to the performance and welfare of their classmates. The threat of suspension or even expulsion from school is a powerful weapon and one which most schools use reluctantly. Nevertheless, as with ADHD, there appears to be a disturbing trend for reluctant parents and even more reluctant children to seek help from Child and Family Clinics and other similar agencies so that schools can be told an attempt is being made to address the problems of difficult behaviour.

Underachieving children

The causes of underachievement at school are many. Some children suffer social deprivation which impairs their capacity to respond to academic instruction in a classroom setting. Typically such children have a profile of psychometric test results in which their performance abilities are higher than their verbal attainments. Other underachieving children have experienced emotional problems. These may have followed parental discord or even separation, some form of abuse, inconsistent parenting, or unrealistic expectations of the child on the part of the parents. Under-achieving children can sometimes be helped by a variety of intervention techniques including family therapy, psychotherapy and cognitive behavioural therapy.

Psychiatric classification of problem children

The DSM-IV and ICD-10 classification systems have already been referred to in earlier sections. They are the two most widely-used systems at the present time. To categorize children with problems according to a medical model of illness has both advantages and disadvantages. The complexities of elaborate patterns of seemingly disturbed behaviour can be reduced when they are construed as giving a reasonable fit to a label or category of disorder. Intervention techniques can be applied with some degree of confidence and parents and teachers can be given some estimate of outcome. The medical model has influenced thinking for so long that many parents expect to be given a label when they encounter what they perceive as difficult behaviour in their children. Accepting the label means that the child does not have to be regarded as naughty or disobedient and the parents for the most part can feel that they are not to blame for things going wrong.

The major disadvantage of classification is that the problem behaviour is attributed to the child when it should be recognized as belonging to the social system in which the child is living. Systemic family therapy focuses on the dysfunctional character-istics of the family. The functioning of the family is interpreted in terms of the stage it has reached in its life-cycle. A few brief examples will serve to indicate the range of intervention models used in family therapy.

The structural model (Minuchin, 1974) places emphasis on the functioning of boundaries between subsystems within the family, particularly between adults and children. Several approaches to family therapy including the Milan school pay particular attention to patterns of communication within families. Narrative therapy takes account of the child within the family, but places more emphasis on allowing the child and other family members to express and understand the multiplicity of stories and realities which are behind the present problem situation. White (1989) has elaborated techniques to help the child externalize the problem in the context of a narrative approach.

SOME PROBLEMS OF MODERN LIVING

Urban and city environments put considerable constraints on the range of play and leisure activities which children can follow in safety. Television dominates the spare time of many. It has been estimated that by the age of 18 most children will have spent more time watching television than in any other activity besides sleep (Liebert and Sprafkin, 1988). Debate continues over the potentially harmful influences from the exposure to frequent scenes of violence. Unfortunately children from socially and emotionally deprived backgrounds get the least encouragement to watch the more educationally-oriented television programmes.

Parents and carers have to take greater measures than in the past to create a protective environment. The decline of the extended family leaves many children with few role models and caring adults within the family. Of the order of one in four children spend at least part of their school-age years in a one-parent household. Many children have parents who are unemployed, whereas others live in considerable affluence.

Environmental pollution is a health hazard for some children. Food additives give rise to allergies in some cases. Air pollution from motor vehicles may be associated with increases in asthma attacks. Nevertheless levels of medical care for children are much higher than in the past.

MEETING PROBLEMS IN THE FUTURE

We can only speculate whether workers in the caring professions will become more effective in the future in the management of problem behaviour in children. The starting point must lie in prevention rather than intervention. We should not be complacent about our childcare standards; in particular there is a need to address the current ambivalence over the commitment on the part of many adults to provide a stable environment and continuity of care for children. Changes in attitude to the rearing of children need to begin as early as the childhood of the present generation if they are to take effect. It may be possible to begin this process of change by giving more attention to the teaching of childcare, home-management and parenting skills in the school curriculum. There is a surprising coyness about presenting such topics to academically able children and adolescents. More controversially, it can be argued that there should be an attempt to include a focus on the importance of mutual respect in caring relationships. Children – young boys in particular – must be helped to refrain from the use of violence. It will not be easy for experts from the different health, welfare and caring professions to agree on an approach and a core curriculum acceptable to educationalists, politicians and theologians. There exists a justifiable fear of anything perceived as approaching social or behavioural engineering. Others value the concept of the aggressive go-getting personality so much that they would resist change. Tough decisions have to be taken about the quality of life for the community in general. If society continues the drift towards greater violence, and towards exposure of children to violence, then we must not be surprised if children adopt these patterns of violence (Osofsky, 1995).

There is a great need to be vigilant about new patterns of child-exploitation. We have long feared that advertising, especially on television, reaches impressionable minds creating unrealistic expectations of purchasing power in children which go well beyond the incomes of their family. More sinister are the stories of access to pornography on the worldwide web which had seemed such an open gate for enquiring minds. Access to drugs by children and adolescents does not 'just happen': adults are involved in the supply and dealing networks. More effective control will depend upon the resolve of the international community and not just that of national governments.

For the future with visions of genetic engineering we can speculate that some of the more severe problems of childhood associated with disabilities might be less common. However, improving standards of medical care mean that more children with life-threatening conditions will survive. It seems likely, then, that there will be increased requirements for special educational needs provision for children with chronic medical problems. Already in some parts of the world HIV encephalopathy may have become the commonest cause of childhood dementia (Thompson, Westwell and Viney, 1994). It is feared that as the proportion of adult heterosexual infection with the HIV virus increases in the developed countries there will be an increase in congenitally infected children. Not all of these children will develop AIDS; nevertheless, the reports of what has already happened in other parts of the world make chilling reading.

Finally we can only speculate on social conditions in the future. Probably more children will live for part of their lives in reconstituted families. Possibly parental age will be older as more couples put off having children until they are established in careers. The demands of education in an increasingly technological age will be greater than ever before. In many ways the world will be even more child-centred than it is now. We must guard against repeating the mistakes of earlier generations by being vigilant about exploitation and by fostering the principles of the need for continuity in care and affection. Melton (1995) draws attention to the importance of dialogue between professionals and those in government to achieve coherence in the areas of child and family policy.

REFERENCES

American Psychiatric Association (1994) *Diagnostic and Statistical Manual of Mental Disorders*, (4th edn). Washington: APA.

Bowlby, J. (1951) *Maternal Care and Mental Health*. Geneva: World Health Organization.

Bowlby, J. (1969) *Attachment and Loss. Volume 1 Attachment*. London: Hogarth Press.

Cunningham, H. (1991) *The Children of the Poor: Representations of Childhood since the Seventeenth Century*. Oxford: Blackwell.

Davie, R., Butler, N. and Goldstein, H. (1972) *From Birth to Seven: A Report on the National Child Development Study*. London: Longman.

DeMause, L. (1974) The evolution of childhood. In L. DeMause (ed.) *The History of Childhood*. New York: Psychohistory Press, pp. 1–73.

DES (1978) *Special Educational Needs*. (The Warnock Report). London: HMSO.

DES (1981) *Education Act*. London : HMSO.

Humphries, S., Mack, J. and Perks, R. (1988) *A Century of Childhood*. London: Sidgwick and Jackson.

Jones, D. and Barrett, H. (1993) Class and hatred. In V. Varma (ed.) *How and Why Children Hate: A Study of Conscious and Unconscious Sources*. London: Jessica Kingsley, pp. 155–69.

Liebert, R.M. and Sprafkin, J. (1988) *The Early Window: Effects of Television on Children and Youth* (3rd edn). New York: Pergamon.

Maudsley, H. (1867) *The Physiology and Pathology of the Mind*. London: Macmillan.

Melton, G.B. (1995) Bringing psychology to Capitol Hill: briefings on child and family policy. *American Psychologist*, **50**, No. 9, 776–70.

Minuchin, S. (1974) *Families and family therapy*. Cambridge, MA: Harvard University Press.

Osofsky, J.D. (1995) The effects of exposure to violence on young children. *American Psychologist*, **50**, 9, 782–8.

Parry-Jones, W.L. (1992) Historical research in child and adolescent psychiatry: scope, methods and application. *Journal of Child Psychology and Psychiatry*, **33**, 803–12.

Parry-Jones, W.L. (1995) Historical aspects of mood and its disorders in young people. In I.M. Goodyer (ed.) *The Depressed Child and Adolescent: Developmental and Clinical Perspectives*. Cambridge: Cambridge University Press, pp. 1–25.

Quinton, D. and Rutter, M. (1988) *Parenting Breakdown: The Making and Breaking of Inter-generational Links*. Aldershot: Avebury.

Rutter, M. and Madge, N. (1976) *Cycles of Disadvantage: A Review of Research*. London: Heinemann.

Snowling, M. (1987) *Dyslexia: A Cognitive Developmental Perspective*. Oxford: Blackwell.

Somerville, C.J. (1982) *The Rise and Fall of Childhood*. Beverley Hills: Sage.

Thompson, C., Westwell, P. and Viney, D. (1994) Psychiatric aspects of human immunodeficiency virus in childhood and adolescence. In M. Rutter, E. Taylor and L. Hersov (eds) *Child and Adolescent Psychiatry: Modern Approaches* (3rd edn). Oxford: Blackwell, pp. 711–19.

United Nations General Assembly (1989) *Convention on the Rights of the Child*. Document A/RES/44/25 (12 December).

Vandivert, W. and Vandivert, R. (1974) Past teaching aids in jigsaw puzzles. *Smithsonian*, **5**, 5, 66–73.

White, M. (1989) Externalizing the problem and the re-authoring of lives and relationships. *Dulwich Centre Newsletter*, Summer, 3–21.

White, R., Carr, P. and Lowe, N. (1990) *A Guide to the Children Act 1989*. London: Butterworths.

World Health Organization (1992) *ICD-10: The ICD-10 Classification of Mental Health and Behavioural Disorders: Clinical Descriptions and Guidelines*. Geneva: WHO.

CHAPTER 2

The Psychiatric Treatment of Children with Behaviour Problems

Philip Barker

This chapter will consider principally children whose behaviour is antisocial and/or oppositional. Such children have failed to learn to conform to the patterns of social behaviour expected in the society of which they are a part. In other words, they are developmental disorders, the aspect of development that has gone awry being the learning of appropriate social skill and behaviours.

The 10th edition of the International Classification of Diseases (ICD-10) (World Health Organization, 1992) defines six subgroups of 'conduct disorders':

1 Conduct disorder confined to the family
2 Unsocialized conduct disorder
3 Socialized conduct disorder
4 Oppositional defiant disorder
5 Other conduct disorders
6 Conduct disorder, unspecified.

ICD-10 also has a separate category for 'hyperkinetic conduct disorders', which it classifies as a subgroup of 'hyperkinetic disorders'.

The American Psychiatric Association's *Diagnostic and Statistical Manual of Mental Disorders* (4th edn) (DSM-IV) (1994) considers conduct disorders, oppositional defiant disorders and 'attention-deficit hyperactivity' disorders together in a section entitled 'Attention-deficit and disruptive behavior disorders'. It also distinguishes two types of conduct disorders, those with onset in childhood and those with adolescent onset.

Such efforts to create categories within what is a heterogeneous and wide-ranging collection of behaviour patterns are commendable attempts to bring order out of chaos; yet they are essentially both arbitrary and artificial and have serious limitations, particularly as guides to treatment and prognosis. In reality the behaviour disorders of childhood and adolescence are a very mixed bag of social-behavioural-emotional disorders, which usually have multiple causes. A comprehensive formulation of each case is more important than the assigning of a diagnostic label.

13

What children with behaviour problems do have in common is that the course of their social development has deviated significantly from that considered normal, or at least acceptable, in their community. The causes of such deviation, however, are legion and usually multiple. There is also a wide variety of ways in which failure to conform to society's behavioural norms may be manifested. Classifying these has value for research and for communication among professionals, but the therapist requires an understanding of how – and, if possible, why – the child's social development has gone awry. With this understanding, it may be possible to develop a plan which will enable the young person to return to a more healthy social developmental path.

PREVALENCE

These disorders are the most common of all child psychiatric disorders but, since their aetiology is both complex and varied, the extent to which the psychiatrist's skills and knowledge are required varies from case to case. Effective treatment often requires the participation of a team, of which the psychiatrist is but one member.

In the Isle of Wight study (Rutter, Tizard and Whitmore, 1970) of 10- and 11-year-olds, about 4 per cent of children were found to have conduct disorder symptoms, while a subsequent study in Inner London (Rutter *et al.*, 1975) found a 12 per cent prevalence rate. In the Ontario Child Health Study (Offord *et al.*, 1987), the following were the percentage rates for conduct disorder that were found:

Boys		Girls	
4–11:	6.5	4–11:	1.8
12–16:	10.4	12–16:	4.1
4–16:	8.1	4–16:	2.8

DEFINITION

According to ICD-10, conduct disorders are characterized 'by a repetitive and persistent pattern of dissocial, aggressive or defiant conduct'. This behaviour involves 'major violations of age-appropriate social expectations, and is therefore more severe than ordinary childish mischief or adolescent rebelliousness'. But 'isolated dissocial or criminal acts are not in themselves grounds for the diagnosis'.

We need to distinguish between 'childish mischief' and more serious disorders, a distinction which may or may not be easy. Moreover, research has shown that what may appear as relatively mild behaviour problems in young children, even toddlers, may presage serious problems later.

To understand what the psychiatrist's role may be in the management of behaviourally troubled children we must first consider how these disorders may arise. These disorders illustrate *par excellence* the biopsychosocial nature of so many human troubles. Rarely is it possible to pinpoint one specific cause for a child's antisocial behaviour. Any of the following may be involved.

Constitutional factors

Genetic

Polygenic influences (resulting from the interaction of a number of genes) may contribute to the development of predisposing personality and temperamental characteristics. Both twin and adoption studies suggest a genetic predisposition to adult criminality, though the evidence is less strong in the case of children (Vandenberg *et al.*, 1986, Chapter 10).

Chromosome abnormalities

Chromosome abnormalities associated with impairment of cognitive functioning may indirectly contribute to behavioural problems, as a result of the learning difficulties and problems in social adaptation such children may experience.

Intrauterine disease or damage, birth injury and prematurity

It has long been known that psychiatric disorders generally are more common in children with neurological disorders than in children without such disorders (Rutter, Graham and Yule, 1970). Some of these problems result from injury or disease during pregnancy or during the birth process.

Physical disease and injury

Physical damage to the brain occurring after birth may be associated with an increased risk of the development of antisocial behaviour. Evidence of trauma to the central nervous system has been found to be particularly common among aggressive young people, including juvenile murderers (Lewis *et al.*, 1988).

Lewis (1991) has suggested that severe medical problems affecting the CNS may contribute to hyperactivity, lability of mood and impulsivity, which in turn may predispose to conduct disorder. Socially acceptable behaviour has to be taught, or modelled, by those among whom children grow up and impairment of brain function may impede this process. There may also be an association between epilepsy, especially when this arises from a focus in the temporal lobe, and aggressive behaviour, but how often this is a significant factor is unclear. Lewis (1991) has also pointed out that there appears to be an association between conduct disordered behaviour, on the one hand, and depression, suicidal ideation and attempts, and drug and alcohol abuse on the other.

There is evidence that the origins of many conduct disorders can be discerned very early in life, even at the toddler stage. Sixty per cent of a sample of delinquents incarcerated in secure settings had histories of incarceration in psychiatric hospitals or residential treatment centres earlier in their lives (Lewis and Shanok, 1980).

Temperamental factors

Children's temperaments vary – probably as much as their physical characteristics do (Chess and Thomas, 1984). Some children are more difficult to rear than others and Chess and Thomas (1984) were able to distinguish those temperamental character-istics which, occurring in combination, result in a 'difficult' child, that is, one which presents a greater challenge to the parents than other children are likely to do. They also suggested that how far they actually do so may depend in part on the 'goodness of fit' between the temperamental styles of the child and of the parents. A clash of temperaments may be the basis of difficulties that become serious and long-lasting. On the other hand, some parents manage to rear successfully children who have strikingly difficult temperaments.

Learning problems

There is a well established association between learning – particularly reading – problems and antisocial behaviour. Whether one causes the other, or whether both are due to common factors, seems to vary from child to child. In any case, if learning problems or academic failure are present, these need to be tackled as part of a comprehensive treatment plan.

Environmental factors

The family

The family (or alternative setting) in which a child is reared is of great importance in influencing personality development and behaviour. In most industrialized western cultures it is the nuclear family's task to rear and socialize its children, though in some other cultures the extended family plays a major role. Children who lack a permanent and stable family group in which to grow up are liable to suffer grave disadvantages.

Fortunately the days of the large impersonal orphanage are past, at least in most western societies. Many children deprived of a normal family life, however, experience repeated moves from one home to another. Those most likely to do so may be those who are most vulnerable because of their 'difficult' temperaments or other biological factors. Frequent moves may adversely affect the process of socialization. The emo-tional attachment to care-givers, an important basis for development, may be im-paired when consistent parent figures are not available. Children whose care-givers often change lack consistent and stable figures with whom to identify. Children who have been 'in care' earlier in childhood have been found to show significantly more deviant, especially antisocial, behaviour later (Wolkind and Rutter, 1973).

The characteristics of families most likely to be successful in rearing their children are quite well established. They include:

- established 'house rules' – set routines and expectations for meals and other activities, and clarity about how the children are expected to behave;
- proper monitoring of the children's behaviour and feelings;
- provision of effective contingencies – consistent and appropriate responses to both desired and undesired behaviour;

- use of techniques with which to deal with crises or problems in the family. (See Patterson (1982) for discussion of these issues.)

Wilson (1980) found weak parental supervision to be the factor most strongly associated with delinquency. Poorly supervised children roam the streets without their parents knowing where they are; they do not know when they are supposed to be home; and they engage in many activities independently of their families.

Dysfunctional parenting may take many forms, not all of which are susceptible to the ministrations of psychiatrists. When the parents are suffering from affective disorders such as depression or mania, or from psychotic conditions, or any other treatable psychiatric disorder, psychiatric intervention may, however, be valuable.

Behaviour problems may be associated with child abuse and/or neglect. The psychopathology of such families is often complex and the psychiatrist may be able to assist in its elucidation and, on occasion, in its amelioration. Other approaches to the improvement of family functioning to which psychiatrists may be able to contribute are to be found in *Basic Family Therapy* (Barker, 1992, especially Chapters 5 and 10).

Extrafamilial factors

These comprise the school, the wider social setting of family and school, and the child's peer group. Dramatic changes in children's behaviour and progress, for better or for worse, may follow a change of school or, sometimes, even a change of teacher or class.

In adolescence, peer group pressures and dynamics may contribute to the genesis of antisocial behaviour.

The interaction of factors

The causative factors discussed above generally interact in complex ways. Temperament seems to be in part genetically determined but may be modified by environmental factors. Physical disease may lead to adverse parental attitudes, and the 'goodness of fit' between child and environment may be a crucial issue . . . and so on.

DESCRIPTION

Children with conduct disorders display what ICD-10 describes as 'a repetitive and persistent pattern of dissocial, aggressive, or defiant conduct'. Symptoms often first become evident within the family group, often as early as the pre-school years, though not all 'naughty' behaviour in young children presages serious behaviour problems later. Relationships with adult authority figures tend to be poor.

As the disorder progresses, the antisocial behaviours may be manifest in an increasingly wide range of situations, for example truancy from school, staying out late, stealing, fire-setting and other delinquent behaviours. In some children it is oppositional behaviour, and the refusal to comply with the reasonable demands of parents, teachers and other adults in their lives that is the main problem area. Drug abuse is also common among children with conduct disorders, especially adolescents, though younger children are not immune.

Deviant sexual behaviour may also be associated with other conduct disorder symptoms, though sometimes it is found on its own.

Juvenile delinquency is more a legal term than a clinical one and is usually applied to the commission of offences that are against the law. This is seen in many troubled children.

ASSOCIATED CONDITIONS

It is often found that children with behaviour problems have other associated problems. These include *attention-deficit hyperactivity disorder* (ADHD) (as described in DSM-IV) and *hyperkinetic disorders* (ICD-10). Sometimes they suffer from *tics*, that is, repetitive involuntary movements such as eye-blinking, head-shaking, facial grimacing, and sudden movement of the limbs. When these are combined with *vocal tics*, the involuntary uttering of sounds or words, which are sometimes obscenities, the condition is called Gilles de la Tourette's syndrome, after the physician who originally described the condition. The combination of tics and ADHD is not uncommon. Tics may also be associated with obsessive-compulsive disorders. Fuller descriptions of these conditions may be found in *Basic Child Psychiatry* (Barker, 1995).

Other associations include reading disability (Rutter, Tizard and Whitmore, 1970; Rutter *et al.*, 1975), depression (Puig-Antich, 1982); and various affective disorders (Marriage *et al.*, 1986).

THE PSYCHIATRIST'S ROLE IN TREATMENT

Behaviourally troubled children have failed to learn to live in harmony with the society of which they are part and their treatment must be based on the best possible understanding of how their difficulties have arisen and, especially, of what is maintaining them. In the more complex cases the assessment and treatment is probably best carried out by a team of which the psychiatrist should be a member.

It will be clear, from the summary above of how children's behavioural problems may arise, that some of the possible aetiological factors are more susceptible to the kinds of treatment that psychiatrists may be able to offer than others, so the psychiatrist's role will vary greatly from case to case. It may also differ depending upon the role the particular psychiatrist plays in the team or programme that is responsible for the young person's assessment and treatment. Psychiatrists are not all the same and each of us, when working as part of a clinical team, tends to find a role that meets the needs of the team of which we are a part. The following are the main roles which the psychiatrist may play.

In assessment

A proper, in-depth assessment is an essential prerequisite for the development of a rational treatment plan. The psychiatrist can play a major part in this. The following main areas are those in which psychiatric expertise can be of value.

In the general medical assessment of the child

This may include taking the medical and psychiatric history, appraising this, and assessing the significance of whatever information comes to light. The psychiatrist may or may not carry out a physical examination of the child though, whether this is done by the psychiatrist or by another physician, this should always be a part of the assessment process. Whether or not referral to another specialist, for example a paediatrician or paediatric neurologist, is indicated is another area in which the psychiatrist may be able to advise.

In determining whether there is a co-existing specific psychiatric disorder

We have seen that depression and other affective disorders may be present in behaviourally troubled children and adolescents. In determining whether this is the case, a comprehensive psychiatric assessment is necessary. Other conditions that may come to light in the course of the psychiatrist's examination include ADHD, tics, anxiety disorders, adjustment disorders and, less often, psychotic and pervasive developmental disorders. Young people, even pre-adolescent children, are also not immune to alcohol and other drug addictions; indeed the sniffing of glue and other inhalants (solvents and petrol, for example) are not uncommon accompaniments of other behavioural problems, especially in certain social groups.

In assessing the mental state of the parents or other care-givers

The parents of some troubled children prove to have serious psychiatric problems of their own. These may be depression or other affective disorders; drug and alcohol addiction; psychotic conditions including schizophrenia; personality disorders; anxiety disorders; adjustment disorders; and other less common conditions.

Recently attention has been increasingly given to 'adult attention-deficit disorder'. It has become apparent that some young people with attention-deficit hyperactivity disorder do not grow out of this by the time they reach adulthood. Since this condition tends to run in families, it is not uncommon to find that a parent with persisting attentional problems is having difficulty dealing consistently and rationally with a child who may have a similar condition. The same may apply to parenting children with other types of problem.

In assessing whether there is an indication for the use of medication

While behaviour problems themselves are not usually susceptible to pharmacological treatment, some of the conditions that may be associated often are. The two classes of drugs most likely to be required are those 'stimulant' drugs which are often effective with children who have attention-deficit hyperactivity disorders; and anti-depressant drugs which may be indicated when there is evidence of associated depression.

In treatment

In monitoring the ongoing use of medication when this is required

In the treatment of psychiatric disorders that come to light in the parents and which appear to be having adverse effects on their parenting skills.

This may include the use of psychotropic drugs or of psychotherapy. In certain cases, however the child psychiatrist may deem it more appropriate to refer the parent to a psychiatrist or other mental health professional with special expertise in the treatment of the disorder in question. This is often the case when admission to hospital is required.

In effecting liaison with other physicians who may be involved in the management of child, parents or the family as a whole

This may be the family physician, paediatrician, paediatric neurologist, other paediatric subspecialist, or general psychiatrist who may be involved with one or more family members.

In addition to these rather specifically medical/psychiatric functions, many psychiatrists have specific skills which may have application as a part of the team effort which is often needed in these cases. These include family therapy skills; individual or group therapy expertise; knowledge of behaviour therapy techniques; and training in hypnotherapy and other special areas.

SPECIFIC THERAPEUTIC NEEDS OF BEHAVIOURALLY TROUBLED CHILDREN

Medication

Drug treatment has a limited role to play in the treatment of conduct disorders, unless there are associated conditions such as epilepsy, attention-deficit hyperactivity disorder, depressive disorder, tics, or a psychotic condition.

The proper control of epilepsy is important regardless of whether there are associated behaviour problems. It may or may not result in improvement in the child's behaviour.

Occasionally it may be necessary to use tranquillizers such as phenothiazine drugs or haloperidol to control acutely and violently aggressive young people, but in properly staffed hospital units and other treatment centres this should rarely be necessary.

As a general rule, medication is not an effective treatment for conduct disorders. Indeed their use has a number of drawbacks. The 'artificial' control of symptoms by medication may preclude the possibility of teaching the necessary skills to parents, child and others who may be involved. When symptoms are pharmacologically repressed it may be hard to work constructively on them. Yet another possible complication is that the use of medication may give the young person and other family members the message that there is a 'magical' pharmacological solution to their problems. This can lead any or all concerned to the erroneous conclusion that they do not need to be as actively involved in the therapeutic effort as in reality they do. So often the main need is for the learning of new social skills, the incorporation of new values and beliefs, the acquisition of improved relationship skills and, usually, changes in the way the family system functions. Ever present also are the danger that drug dependence may develop and the risk of undesired side effects. For example, while it may be possible to achieve some control over aggressive behaviour by the use of tranquillizing drugs, this is often at the cost of some sedation which may impair the child's school performance.

Individual psychotherapy

The role of individual psychotherapy, which is something the psychiatrist may provide, is generally quite limited in treatment of these children. It is seldom that the child or adolescent is the one who is complaining – though some troubled young people are seeking to change their behaviour. The reluctance to acknowledge the existence or severity of their problems, which is often encountered in working with behaviourally troubled young people, may limit their interest in attending for therapy sessions. Moreover treatment, as we have seen, usually has to take into account the wider context of the child's problems. Furthermore, certain young people seem to be getting some vicarious satisfaction from their defiant or antisocial behaviour.

Despite the above considerations, there is a minority of children who have a high level of consciously-felt anxiety, or are motivated in some other way, and who can be helpfully engaged in psychotherapy. This group includes some abused children, and those who have a strong conscious desire to change their way of life because it has led them into situations which they have found unwelcome.

Many children displaying antisocial behaviour have low levels of self-esteem and, in this area also, individual therapy can be of value.

Group psychotherapy

This form of treatment, which again the psychiatrist may be able to provide or participate in, suffers from some of the same limitations as individual therapy. The psychiatrist may play a part in determining which children or young people can benefit from group therapy, and some have a special interest in carrying out group therapy themselves. Despite the limited application of group therapy, groups which enhance the young person's self-esteem, or provide these children with opportunities to learn new social or vocational skills – for example drama, dance, martial arts, ceramics, gymnastics, carpentry or metalworking – can provide significant help. For abused children, participation in a group with other children who have had similar experiences can be powerfully therapeutic.

Residential treatment

This has sometimes been advocated for children with severe conduct disorders, though its results have been quite variable. It may or may not be provided in a hospital or other medical facility, but when it is, the psychiatrist's role is often a major one. The best results seem to be those of centres in which there is a skilled team of mental health professionals from a variety of disciplines and which use well planned and intensive behaviour therapy methods. While considerable improvement in the behaviour of troubled children often occurs when they are placed in structured residential settings and are confronted with strict behavioural controls, this may not be sustained when they return to their homes. Nevertheless residential treatment does have its place, if only for those children who cannot be contained in the community because of the severity of their behaviour problems. In such situations, a psychiatrist should always be available as a resource person to the clinical team, for all the reasons set out above.

Day treatment

This is an alternative to residential treatment and has the advantage that the young person is not separated full-time from the family. When the child is at home in the evenings and at weekends, the family members can practise the skills they are learning in treatment. The availability of psychiatric consultation is as important in day treatment units as it is in in-patient units and other residential settings.

Exactly similar considerations apply to hybrid programmes, such as five-day residential treatment, in which children receive active treatment from Monday to Friday and then spend the weekend at home, progress during that time being reviewed when the parents bring the child back to the treatment setting after the weekend. Some treatment programmes have staff on call during the weekend, so that parents, or children, can telephone them to discuss problems that arise during the weekend.

Other areas in which the psychiatrist may be of assistance

The psychiatrist may act as a consultant and resource person in other areas. These include the treatment of associated conditions, whether in the child or in other family members.

Depression is one of the commonest associations, and in severe cases suicidal ideation or behaviour may complicate it. In managing children showing depression or suicidal tendencies, the active involvement of a psychiatrist may be of particular importance. Moreover, it is sometimes found that behavioural improvement occurs in depressed children with conduct disorder symptoms when the depression resolves, the symptoms returning with recurrence of the depression.

SUMMARY

Clinically significant behaviour disorders in children usually have multiple causes. They are best regarded as disorders of the development of social behaviour and skills. They rarely have a single cause; rather they are the result of the interaction of multiple factors operating over a period of time which often goes back to the pre-school period of life. The inherent personality and temperamental characteristics of the child; the family, school and neighbourhood environments; learning problems; brain damage or disease; abuse and/or neglect; and co-existing psychiatric disorders such as depression – all may contribute.

The study and treatment of these complex disorders require the involvement of a variety of disciplines. These may include social work, family therapy, psychology, education, speech therapy, and other medical specialties, as well as psychiatry. The psychiatrist can, however, usually make important contributions as a consultant to the clinical team and in some cases can participate actively in the therapeutic endeavour, especially in the treatment of coexisting psychiatric disorders, and when medication is required. The psychiatrist may also participate in individual, group or family therapy, depending on his or her particular interests and role in the clinical team.

REFERENCES

American Psychiatric Association (1994) *Diagnostic and Statistical Manual of Mental Disorders* (4th ed). Washington: APA.

Barker, P. (1992) *Basic Family Therapy* (3rd edn). Oxford: Blackwell.

Barker, P. (1995) *Basic Child Psychiatry* (6th edn). Oxford: Blackwell.

Chess, S. and Thomas, A. (1984) *Origins and Evolution of Behaviour Disorders from Infancy to Adult Life*. New York: Brunner/Mazel.

Lewis, D.O. and Shanok, S. (1980) The use of a correctional setting for follow-up care of psychiatrically disturbed adolescents. *American Journal of Psychiatry*, **137**, 953–5.

Lewis, D.O. (1991) Conduct disorder. In M. Lewis (ed.) *Child and Adolescent Psychiatry: A Comprehensive Textbook*. Baltimore: Williams & Wilkins.

Lewis, D.O., Pincus, J.H., Bard, B., Richardson, E., Prichep, L.S., Feldman, M. and Yeager, C. (1988) Neuropsychiatric, psychoeducational and family characteristics of 14 juveniles condemned to death in the United States. *American Journal of Psychiatry*, **145**, 584–9.

Marriage, K., Fine, S., Moretti, M. and Haley, G. (1986) Relationship between depression and conduct disorder in children and adolescents. *Journal of the American Academy of Child Psychiatry*, **25**, 687–91.

Offord, D.R., Boyle, M.H., Szatmari, P., Rae-Grant, N.I., Links, P.S., Cadman, D.T., Byles, J.A., Crawford, J.W., Blum, H.M., Byrne, C., Thomas, H. and Woodward, C.A. (1987) Ontario Child Health Study: prevalence of disorders and rates of service utilization. *Archives of General Psychiatry*, **44**, 832–6.

Patterson, G.R. (1982) *Coercive Family Process*. Eugene, OR: Castilia.

Puig-Antich, J. (1982) Major depression and conduct disorder in puberty. *Journal of the American Academy of Child Psychiatry*, **21**, 118–28.

Rutter, M., Cox, A., Tupling, G., Berger, M. and Yule, W. (1975) Attainment and adjustment in two geographical areas: 1. The prevalence of psychiatric disorder. *British Journal of Psychiatry*, **126**, 493–501.

Rutter, M., Graham, P. and Yule, W. (1970) *A Neuropsychiatric Study on Childhood*. London: Heinemann.

Rutter, M., Tizard, J. and Whitmore, K. (1970) *Education, Health and Behaviour*. London: Longman.

Vandenberg, S.G., Singer, S.M. and Pauls, D.L. (1986) *The Heredity of Behaviour Disorders in Adults and Children*. New York: Plenum.

Wilson, H. (1980) Parental supervision: a neglected aspect of delinquency. *British Journal of Criminology*, **20**, 203–35.

Wolkind, S. and Rutter, M. (1973) Children who have been 'in care': an epidemiological study. *Journal of Child Psychology and Psychiatry*, **14**, 97–105.

World Health Organization (1992) *The ICD–10 Classification of Mental and Behavioural Disorders: Clinical Descriptions and Diagnostic Guidelines*. Geneva: WHO.

CHAPTER 3

The Psychological Approach to Assessment: The Child within the Family

Jean Sambrooks and Steve Fuller

Children may develop problems for a variety of reasons and it is important at the outset of the referral to ensure that the therapist explores the whole problem rather than focusing specifically on the child. This chapter looks at the approach adopted by two cognitive behavioural therapists who have worked together with children and parents experiencing difficulties and tries to highlight the issues that they regard as relevant to the assessment process. They would stress however that there is a vast literature concerning children's mental health and it is therefore unlikely that any approach is truly unique but will instead consist of each professional's interpretation of the research coupled with his or her clinical experience and judgement as to the best way of achieving an accurate assessment. What is vital, however, is to remember that the assessment process is the 'lynch-pin' upon which any other work is based and it is therefore important that any assessment is carefully and thoroughly carried out, even though at times this may seem to be pedantic and obsessive from the family's point of view as they struggle to contain the problem.

It is also relevant to comment that children, at least until they are deemed able to give informed consent, have little choice as to whether or not they are referred for assessment or therapy. Children are referred by parents, by schools and by other agencies and are therefore often presented as the focus of the problem; yet any assessment process must be broader than the child even if he or she is the catalyst for the initial assessment.

Children are the product of the genetic endowment they bring to life; of whatever physical and emotional stimulation they encounter throughout their life; and of the family in which they exist, together with the society within which that family unit functions. They are also the product of life circumstances which will impinge upon them to a greater or lesser extent, life circumstances which may be specific to the child or may affect the family or the community and hence affect the child. The purpose of this chapter is to outline the scope of any assessment and will look at the child from the three perspectives of the child, the parents and the child within the family. It looks at the factors to be considered from each angle but makes no assumptions as to which angle will be pursued first. Rather it seeks to highlight the important areas for consideration when making an assessment. It must also be noted that the framework adopted by a therapist may influence whether parent, child or the whole family are seen. Additionally the child's own presenting problem will have influence; for example, a child admitted to hospital with an overdose may initially be seen individually because of the circumstances of his or her admission and only thereafter seen within the family.

The authors also draw on Belsky's model of family functioning which identifies three main influences on people's ability to parent and highlights the importance of the following factors (Belsky, 1984); the psychological resources of the parents, including their own mental health and attachment and developmental history; contextual sources of support such as partners, relatives, friends and current financial and employment circumstances; and the characteristics of the child.

THE CHILD

One aspect of the assessment therefore is to seek to explain those issues which children bring to the process. However, when faced with a period of difficult behaviour and subsequent referral to a system about which they may not previously have known, parents and carers are often unable to describe their children's behaviour other than in general terms. This reflects their own confusion and their concerns that the child's moods and behaviours do not appear to follow any apparent or understandable pattern. Indeed parents may have become increasingly worried that their child is uncontrollable and at this stage, then, it will certainly appear that the child's behaviour is leading any family interaction. The child's problematic behaviour becomes paramount within this system and other family agendas become secondary. Parents thus present as being stuck and unable to cope despite their report that they have 'tried everything'.

In some instances children's behaviour may be the result of, or reaction to, some immediate family stress or trauma such as illness or loss, for example. Childhood behavioural difficulties may also be developmental and transitory and therefore not require regular input; for example, separation anxieties are not uncommon at times of transition from home to playgroup, nor nightmares after trauma.

The authors incorporate a lifespan approach to assessment and will explore the child's current behaviours and the contexts in which they occur. They may well ask about less obvious and immediate consequences such as 'Does the child's present lifestyle prevent them from forming reciprocal and intimate social relationships and from learning effectively at school?' or 'Does the child's behaviour represent a regressive or more permanent trend?' (see Douglas, 1989).

When exploring further and specifically the factors which the child brings to the assessment, one needs to understand the interaction between diverse elements. There are many which must be taken into consideration, including developmental history and cognitive ability, temperament and current behaviours, as well as the child's present relationships and own understanding of his or her difficulties.

A child's temperament underpins the way he or she responds to difficulties. Most human babies, although helpless and dependent, have innate abilities such as responding to their parent(s) or having the capacity to learn, which helps both bonding and the formation of relationships. However, research shows that babies display a distinctive range of different patterns in crying, in sleeping and in their reactions to being soothed. Indeed the work of Thomas and Chess (1977), especially, is recognized for investigating these innate styles of temperament which children bring to their primary relationships. On the basis of interview Thomas and Chess identified clusters of traits which they suggest form two overall groups. **Difficult** babies are both negative in mood and irregular in routine; they seem to be 'criers', poor sleepers and poor feeders. **Easy** babies are those identified as positive and as having patterns of sleep and feeding; they adjust well and respond readily to people; in many ways they are very rewarding to care for.

The assessment process from the child aspect may therefore be seen as a way of exploring the characteristics which each child brings to his or her role within the family. Temperament, however, is neither static nor immutable but will influence (rather than *determine*) the child's reaction to particular stressors or events, as will also the family's subsequent style of coping.

In a child, adolescent and family clinical psychology department, 10 to 20 per cent of the cases seen may have been arbitrarily identified as 'emotional' and 'behavioural/conduct' difficulties (Kurtz 1992). However, emotional difficulties may also be re-ferred as depression, fears, phobias and reactions to separation and loss. Similarly, conduct disorders may be also referred as aggression, theft and defiance. In practice, however, many children will present with aspects of both. (For example, a child's response to parental separation may well include depression and aggression.)

Therefore assessing the presence and significance of 'so-called' behavioural and/or emotional difficulties from the child's perspective is the first step in identifying whether further input is warranted. Indeed, Rutter (1975) suggests it is important to bear in mind the following four parameters:

- the degree and suffering which a child experiences. For example, a child who appears shy may actually be composed and self sufficient; conversely, he or she may be depressed and unable to communicate further.
- the social restriction the problem engenders. For example, encopretic children often miss out on other children's birthday parties or cub/brownie camp and therefore may not learn the requisite skills needed for social interaction.
- the extent to which the problem interferes with development. Phobic children may also lack exposure to appropriate peer relationships and hence may not develop autonomy outside of the family.
- the effect of the problem on other people. It may cause family relationships to become tailored to the child's needs rather than to those of siblings, or the whole family may experience distress or isolation.

To illustrate this framework it may be useful to look further at some examples of the most common problems which children bring to the assessment process, although this is by no means an exhaustive list.

Studies suggest an association between language difficulties and behaviour prob-lems in young children (Stevenson and Richman, 1978). This is commonly viewed as being the result of frustration for children who cannot put their needs and wants across. It may also show an inability to understand and respond to the demands of a verbal environment. Such children are often reprimanded for non-compliance, or compared unfavourably to their more verbally sophisticated peers or siblings. The child's communicative deficits may subsequently lead to a slower development of social skills and peer relationships and consequent impaired self-esteem and associated emotional and behaviour problems (Bishop, 1994).

Many children with developmental difficulties also come to the notice of clinical psychologists. Children with such problems will often have a range of associated difficulties which need to be further and fully assessed within a holistic framework involving other mental health disciplines as well as the local authority. The pervasive developmental disorders are characterized by severe difficulties in communication and behaviour and, especially, in an inability to develop reciprocal social relationships. There are often associated medical and cognitive difficulties (see Gillberg, 1990). While there is no known cure, for example, for the subtypes autism or Asperger's syndrome, a multiple treatment approach is currently the most promising. This would involve assessments and input at both an individual and contextual level to take into account the child's needs in communication, social skills and education as well as offering support and advice to parents and family members. Many pervasive difficulties may thus incorporate all four of Rutter's criteria.

Up to 40 per cent of mental health referrals may be for children having attention deficit hyperactivity disorder (ADHD). Definitions may be somewhat variable, however, and clear diagnosis is important (see Taylor, 1985). Presenting behaviours frequently contain restless, impulsive and overactive elements. Hence, a school may identify a child who has difficulty waiting turns, who is intrusive and who generally moves around all the time. Such a child also appears selective regarding his or her attention and abilities. Care-givers will often describe a child who cannot play, who is disobedient, aggressive and who is constantly 'on the go'. Parents may typically not understand why their child behaves in this way, when they feel that they have tried everything; children may well feel that they are constantly being reprimanded, teased, or held up for attention. While the family will require support and advice, the child too will need individual therapeutic input to enhance both self-esteem and confidence as well as instruction on how to increase his or her attention span.

As with many referred difficulties, childhood problems of elimination also cover a broad continuum ranging from simple urinary frequency to chronic encopresis and enuresis. They can be both common and very distressing in themselves, as well as having quite profound consequences; for example, until toilet-trained, children may be excluded from school or from social gatherings, parties and 'sleepovers'. Children may be mocked by their peers or siblings and may also present difficulties within fostering and adoption facilities. Lastly, caregivers may often admit to physical forms of punishment in the more severe and chronic cases. In addition the problem may extend beyond the initial elementary problems and such children can become quite isolated as a result of their lack of socialization and miss out on further opportunities to engage in and learn appropriate social interaction.

The section above highlights some of the issues surrounding the problems that children bring to the assessment process. However, families often may feel that they are alone with their problems, as mental health issues are infrequently acknowledged and may even be disregarded. This latter point may also hold true for many of the issues which children bring to the assessment process, as too often parents and children may feel that they are labelled as 'failures', for example.

THE PARENTS

The second strand of the assessment process considers the contribution of the parents to the development of the child's perceived problems. Parents bring to parenting and to the development of their children's potential a whole range of skills, strengths and knowledge, and also current and historical difficulties. These are considered below and must be taken into account at the outset in order to best determine the therapist's subsequent input.

Parents' own experience as children

One important aspect to consider is the impact of a person's experiences of being parented as this significantly influences their own ability to parent. If parents have never experienced the full development of their own potential by other adults (whether by listening to and playing with them, by nurturing and protecting them, by providing materials and opportunities), then their knowledge of how to fulfil this function for their own child may be limited (Garbarino *et al.*, 1986). While parents can gain information from books, from television or from other people, there is little substitute for one's own experiences of parenting, and the impact of teaching devices is variable. Indeed without a base line of attachment experience upon which to impose other sources of information, then learning to parent becomes an enormous task. While the amount of attention and stimulation applied to the parents as children may govern the extent to which they can fulfil their own child's need for stimulation and attention, the parents' experience of abuse as children may also affect their parenting skills. The research literature indicates that abuse, whether physical, emotional (Garbarino *et al.*, 1986) or sexual (Finkelhor, 1986), may have considerable effects upon the survivor's parenting skills, although the authors would not wish to suggest that this was always the case. However, a small percentage of parents who have been abused as children may themselves, despite their acknowledgement of the problem, go on to abuse or to link with partners who abuse their children. (Finkelhor, 1986). This becomes yet another facet to be kept in mind when assessing the parent's possible contribution to the child's problem.

Parents' own abilities and needs

Parents also come to the task of parenting with their own genetic make-up and cognitive abilities and some parents may be more able than others to understand the diverse tasks of parenting. Intellectual difficulties do not themselves mean that the parents cannot parent successfully with or without advice from external sources, but a combination of parents' abilities and their individual needs may make them more or less receptive to external advice as regards parenting or may make it difficult for them to recognize the appropriateness of their own actions. One author recalls working with a parent who was fond of her child but felt that, because the pre-school child was able to walk and talk and in that sense express himself, then he was also able to take responsibility for his own behaviour. Hence when the child indicated that he wished to go for a walk the parent would allow him that choice but not understand the need to accompany him nor appreciate the child's relative understanding of traffic conditions, strangers, danger, etc. Similarly she would only feed him when he said he was hungry! While no intentional harm was intended to the child, the exposure to risk might well create a situation that subsequently affected both the child and the family. In another family the mother well understood the child's physical needs and was a very capable mother in this respect. However her own childhood experiences were such that she lacked any appropriate attachment figure and was therefore herself very needy for affection and attention. She thus had no understanding of her child's emotional needs for affection and attention and as a consequence the child had become aggressive and developed a soiling problem.

Parental health

Parental health, both physical and psychological, will add to or detract from the parents' ability to meet their children's needs, to recognize the difficulties their children have or to cope with those problems, and this has to be taken into account when assessing what approach to offer a family presenting with difficulties. Such issues need to be explored either from the parents' or the children's viewpoint. From the parents' perspective, one facet of the problem may be the parents' guilt or distress and their own inability to meet their children's needs. From the children's perspective, it may be necessary to help them come to terms with and recognize their parents' problems and the effects those may have upon them. These issues may be expressed by the children in fears and anxieties concerning their own or their parents' future; may be shown by anger or hostility emanating from the children in respect of their parents' inability to set aside their own problems; or may result in a rejection of parental values, etc. as an expression of the children's distress or hostility at real or perceived injustice.

An exploration of the parents' own attachment experiences of being parented is therefore clearly significant in determining how they relate to others and how they meet their child's own needs. Maternal depression, particularly following the birth of a child, is also well documented in the literature as a feature of attachment disorders (Field *et al.*, 1988). This may later present as the child's problems but in effect has developed from the parents' own depression. Maternal depression is common in isolated families particularly in low-income, inner-city areas and it has been estimated that as many as 30 per cent of mothers in this situation suffer from depression (Brown and Harris, 1978). The effects of depression are to make the parents less responsive to their children's needs, less able to meet the children's attachment needs, less able to bond with them and less able to meet their physical and emotional needs for care and stimulation, etc., which in turn can produce a variety of reactions in the children. Such information is vital when planning an effective treatment package that the *family* can feel able to adopt.

Other parental and external factors

Parents also bring a host of personal factors with them to any assessment. Parents may bring significant pieces of information as they have a knowledge of their child far beyond that which the professional gains at interview; they can provide help and understanding for their child. They bring with them differing skills with which to cope with the demands of the situation and this is itself a significant factor when assessing what advice to offer, as parents may have different abilities when working with professionals which will stem from a variety of sources.

Parents may feel guilt if they consider themselves in any way responsible for the development and maintenance of the problem; vulnerable because they are aware that the child has problems that they do not seem able to understand or resolve themselves; anger, particularly if they see the child, or society, as being responsible for the current difficulties or confusion because of external factors to do with health or education services. An assessment of the parents' ability to work with professionals is therefore of considerable importance at this stage. The sensitivity and skill of the professional in considering these issues are crucial factors in the success of any intervention and may determine whether the family is *able* to accept the advice and help offered, from whichever perspective – child, parents, or the family – is assessed as being the main problem area.

External factors can also have considerable influence upon a family and on children with the family. Children who have not previously shown any difficulties may develop problems following on from external events; or the parents'/family's reaction to these circumstances may itself result in the children exhibiting difficulties. If one takes the example of a traumatic event, be it an accident or a disaster, then these external factors can have a profound effect upon children and their families. Indeed the authors' experience in assessing a number of families involved in a traumatic coach accident clearly highlighted the diverse effects trauma can have upon various families. In this incident one child was tragically and quite horrifically killed, one child on the coach was severely injured and, while the other children in the main were not physically injured, the trauma was considerable. The psychological effects were influenced by such variables as whether the children were separated at the time from their parents; whether the children witnessed the tragedy or were only aware of an event but not the nature of it; whether the children knew the victim closely; and the children's and their parents' own personal reaction to the trauma. Some children thereafter were traumatized at the idea of travelling again by coach. Other children had little difficulty with this but their parents had great difficulty *allowing* them to travel by coach, which then impinged upon the children's freedom to travel on school trips, affected their own well-being within peer groups or caused them to develop problems with their school and peer groups. The family of the child who was injured had to come to terms with the trauma of being involved in medical treatment in a country where they did not speak the language and did not understand the situation, the slow recovery of their child and the changed nature of his presentation after the trauma – which one parent reacted to with distress and the other with anger and irritation with consequent interpersonal conflict. It can therefore be seen that the consequences of such a trauma may have a profound effect upon children and parents and also upon parent-child and parent-parent relationships, resulting in the development of closer positive relationships or the increasing separation and disintegration of the parents' own relationship or of the family as each person struggles to cope with the trauma of the event.

How parents cope with life circumstances such as unemployment, housing difficulties, bereavement depends to some extent on the support available to them. This is often significant in determining whether or not a child who is presenting with a difficulty is perceived as having a problem or whether the problem is contained or resolved within the family. On a simple level, when a single parent is experiencing a problem with a child's sleeping regime, then the family situation can very easily become fraught. The parent becomes significantly over-tired and perhaps becomes negative towards the child, who may then respond with either withdrawal behaviour or his or her own negative behaviour as they both struggle to make sense of what is happening to them. If support is available in terms of a supportive partnership, extended families and statutory and voluntary agencies, then the parent may be assisted in (for example) gaining sleep at alternative times or in trying alternative and positive approaches to problem-solving. In turn the parent and child may then be free to enjoy their relationship and possibly prevent further difficulties.

THE CHILD WITHIN THE FAMILY

The third aspect of the assessment process to be considered is that of the child within the family. By and large, across cultures, most 'good enough' parents and carers intuitively seem to meet their children's mental health needs out of their affection and their concern. Among the basic requirements which are thus met are physical care; affection; security; the stimulation of innate potential; and guidance and control (see Pringle, 1975).

With these as the building blocks for child mental health, diverse schemata have been proposed to further understand the development of potential and of relationships throughout the lifespan (e.g. Erikson, 1968). Some of the factors which they have in common are an increasing autonomy, an awareness of other people and their feelings and a developing sense of reciprocal interaction. Parents similarly have these goals and expectations of self-actualization for their children.

Given, then, that many of these skills for an understanding of the social world are developed through the family, the authors feel it is important to look at the parenting skills offered within the family to the child in question; to consider how parents foster this particular child's psychological development; and what influence this may have had on the development of the referred 'problem' behaviours. Adults respond to both behaviours and needs, for example, by comforting a crying baby. However, specific aspects of one baby as distinct from those of its sibling (e.g. colour of hair, resemblance to violent partner, etc.) may make the parents less able to respond in this way to *that* child, and thus indicating a factor that needs further exploration.

When offering an assessment, the authors also explore the role that significant 'others' play in the development of social behaviour and interactional skills. Children learn some behaviours through modelling (observational learning) and the parents' and other family members' behaviour may therefore have contributed to the problem referred. However, a child's phobia of fire, for example, may develop in the absence of any modelling of fear and presents the parents with an enigma specific to that child.

Parents also instruct children. Within the field of child mental health, it is often acknowledged that parents/caregivers work within behaviour management guidelines and ideologies about children's behaviour. They both teach and modify, but without a thorough knowledge of the theoretical background. However a child with ADHD may require significantly greater skill or may be unresponsive to those strategies effective with siblings or peers. Such children may instead modify their parents' behaviour to the detriment of their own development.

Attribution theory identifies how cause and effect can be communicated to children via family rules, fables or traditional children's stories. Meanings and consequences of actions are thus conveyed but may be reinterpreted by the brighter child to his or her own egocentric advantage. Similarly, a chaotic family with few boundaries may fail to provide such teaching. Again the child's own characteristics are relevant and the temperamentally passive child may allow such rules to go unchallenged, whereas the child with challenging behaviour or an aggressive temperament may identify discrepancies within the rules.

By providing them with encouraging settings, parents enable children to learn how to explore and to play with peers. The extent to which parents encourage their children to attend playgroups and mix with others outside of the family home is therefore important. However, the withdrawn child will not respond to such situations as peers and siblings do. Separation anxiety is a two-way process.

Given the need to take all the aforementioned factors into account, any assessment should become a collaborative relationship. The Clinical Psychologist joins with both the child and the parents to try to understand their present functioning and the nature of the difficulties they are encountering. This assessment in itself becomes part of the process of empowering the family to communicate and to change. The assessment should therefore also seek to identify people's capacity for therapeutic input and begin to investigate exactly what their expectations are of Child, Adolescent and Mental Health services. For example, what are parents and children looking for? Are they the same and are these age-appropriate and realistic?

However, as well as addressing the preceding issues in respect of the child, the parents and the child within the family, the assessment needs to progress to consider the areas set out below.

SUMMARY OF ASSESSMENT PROCESS

Initially the clarification of the problem and its associated parameters, should be sought. All parties can be involved in this aspect of assessment, as it helps for everyone (including the child) to be aware of the reasons for referral. This process may itself begin to involve people in communicating with each other, hence possibly facilitating change.

Typical questions at this stage may revolve around reaching agreements on what exactly is it that the child does, under what conditions and with whom? It may also be useful at this time to offer an A–B–C formulation to the family and ask them to keep some form of appropriate and mutually understandable record.

The developmental and psychological history of the child must also be identified. Children's reactions to trauma (such as illness, separation and loss) can be both severe and far-reaching. Assessment needs to both acknowledge this with all members of the family system while also engaging the young person, the parent and the family for future therapy. Similarly, assessment needs to ascertain everyone's present abilities in order to help best determine the most appropriate resources and input.

Besides looking at existing and future supports and, for example, people's capacity for containment, the assessment interview can also explore other influences upon the child and the family within the system, such as access to drugs or alcohol, while a genogram may be helpful at this initial stage.

Finally it may be too easy to be seduced into a family's desperate view of their child; parents and professionals, as well as the child, need to be reminded that the child is more than a description of problematic behaviours and attitudes. To identify the positive attributes not only gives a balanced focus but also acknowledges areas that can be maintained and acts as a reminder of the child's strengths. The authors remember sadly one family who, despite considering the issues for a week, failed to identify one positive attribute in their child, interpreting even significant positive behaviour in a negative fashion.

In effect, then, the assessment process seeks to determine the origins of the development of a problem; the factors contributing to its maintenance; those parts of the family that can work with change and by this process suggest an appropriate and therefore – one hopes – successful therapeutic focus. However, it must be remembered that families do not live only within their extended family structure and their local sociocultural environment, but also within their cultural heritage. Such factors will also have implications for the family's perception of the problem.

REFERENCES

Belsky, J. (1984) The determinants of parenting: a process model. *Child Development*, **55**, 83–96.

Bishop, D.V.M. (1994) Developmental disorders of speech and language. In M. Rutter, E.A. Taylor, and L.A. Hersov (eds) *Child and Adolescent Psychiatry, Modern Approaches*. Oxford: Blackwell Scientific Publications, pp. 546–68.

Brown, G. and Harris, T. (1978) *Social Origins of Depression*. London: Tavistock.

Douglas, J. (1989) *Behaviour Problems in Young Children*. London: Routledge.

Erikson, E. (1968) *Identity: Youth and Crisis*. London: Faber.

Field, T., Healy, B., Goldstein, S., Percy, S., Bendell, D., Schanberg, S., Zimmerman, E.A. and Duhn, C. (1988) Infants of deprived mothers show 'depressed' behaviour even with non-depressed adults. *Child Development*, **59**, 1569–79.

Finkelhor, D. (1986) *A Source Book on Childhood Sexual Abuse*. London: Sage.

Garbarino, J., Guttman, E. and Feeley, J.W. (1986) *The Psychologically Battered Child*. San Francisco: Jossey Bass.

Gillberg, C. (1990) Autism and pervasive developmental disorders. *Journal of Child Psychology and Psychiatry*, **31**, 99–110.

Kurtz, Z. (ed.) (1992) *With Health in Mind: Mental Health Care for Children and Young People*. London: Action for Sick Children.

Pringle, M.K. (1975) *The Needs of Children*. London: Hutchinson.

Rutter, M. (1975) *Helping Troubled Children*. Harmondsworth: Penguin.

Stevenson, J. and Richman, N. (1978) Behaviour, language and development in three-year-old children. *Journal of Autism and Childhood Schizophrenia*, **8**, 299–313.

Taylor, E.A. (1985) *The Hyperactive Child: A Parent's Guide*. London: Dunitz.

Thomas, A. and Chess, S. (1977) *Temperament and Development*. New York: Bruner/Mazel.

CHAPTER 4

A Systemic Behavioural Approach for Children with Problems

Hitesh Raval

INTRODUCTION

Children lead their daily lives in numerous contexts or environments (e.g. home, school, nursery, community, society). Some of their behaviour will be consistent across different contexts or environments. The context may determine how the child's behaviour is defined, as will the person defining the behaviour. For example, a fourteen-year-old child going up to an adult and giving them a hug will be seen as appropriate in the home or social environment when the adult is known to the child. However, this same behaviour may be seen as inappropriate with an adult with whom the child has a different relationship (e.g. the child hugging a teacher in front of the other pupils at school). A stranger watching the child hug someone on the street may define this behaviour as 'delinquent and immoral'. The child's parent watching this may observe their child greeting a close relative. The manner in which people talk to each other will create a 'meaning' for what has been observed. This socially constructed meaning can then take on the quality of being the truth about what has been observed (White, 1989).

In professional settings the child is often brought along for help when an important adult in his or her life has defined the child's behaviour as problematic. The child may or may not be aware of the reasons or the label that has brought him or her to the attention of an outside agency. Professionals will create their own version of the truth in order to understand the problem being presented to them. The adults bringing the child along for the 'painless magical fix' will give over some of their power to the professionals so that they can carry out their magic. Within all of this the child usually has the least amount of power, while all the adults debate what to do to the child to make everything better again. The professionals therefore have to think very carefully about what the problem is, and for whose benefit change is being sought. The professionals also have to decide about the most appropriate type of help needed by the child and the adults referring the child, and where this help can best be provided if the professionals or their particular service are unable to provide it. In order to understand the nature of the problem the professionals have to decide which meaning (or truth), or whose meaning, is the most useful in being able to help the referred system achieve the desired change that is being sought. Often the assumption is that the referring adults know what is in the best interests of the child, and hence are the ones who can define the change that is to be worked towards. The professionals have to address these issues of power imbalances and develop a way of negotiating 'change goals' that are of benefit to the child as much as to the adults in the child's life. Issues involved with negotiating a behavioural contract with families and the process by which this can be done constructively have been discussed by Crane (1995).

THE CHILD'S BEHAVIOUR IN CONTEXT

The child can be understood in many ways. One way of understanding the child is by placing them within their contexts. Each context can be thought of as one level in which to think about a child's behaviour. Useful levels at which to understand a child's behaviour include the societal context, the community context, the family context, the individual level, the behavioural level, the child's cognitive level, and other relevant constitutional factors. The way in which the child interacts within these contexts will also be determined to some extent by the child's individual characteristics. Each of these contexts or levels can also be thought of as exerting on-going interactive influences on each other. The above levels provide a starting point from which to understand a child's behaviour and are shown in Figure 4.1.

For example the act of fighting may be seen as a negative behaviour by a child's parents, other family members and the school teachers; but, in a case where the child is getting bullied at school, fighting may be seen as more positive within the child's peer group where being able to stand up to bullies gives added status to the child. Not fighting may lead to further bullying of the child. Consequently this may lead the child to develop a low self-esteem, which is maintained as the child starts to fall behind with school work. The adults are alerted to the problem when they become puzzled about why this child is suddenly falling behind with the academic work. In this instance the school may intervene to stop the bullying. Alternatively, the child standing up to the bully may be enough to change the other children's views, and this change in the other children's perception may be a stronger influence to stop the bullying – and free up the child to function better at school again.

The interactive process by which behaviour and the meaning given to it is influenced by the context has been described by Cronen *et al.* (1982) in their theory of the coordinated management of meaning (CMM theory). They have suggested the following six contexts or hierarchical levels:

1. Cultural Pattern: the general pattern of human behaviour which informs and legitimizes ways of knowing and ways of behaving
2. Life Script: an individual's behavioural repertoire that gives rise to his or her self-concept
3. Relationship: collective understanding of people by each other
4. Episode: complete interaction of a behavioural exchange
5. Speech Acts: the things that we do to each other with words or actions

6. Content: information about anything that is communicated containing no indication of what kind of message it is.

Cronen *et al.* (1982) state that a higher context is needed in order to understand the meaning or function of the context below it. They view each context to have a reciprocal relationship such that each context can simultaneously be a context for and within the context of another. Sometimes a major change in the 'meaning' associated with a lower context can lead to a change in the 'meaning' available in the higher context (i.e. upward or implicative force). Alternatively, a small change in the 'meaning' associated with a higher context can lead to changes in the meaning associated with a lower context (i.e. downward or contextual force).

For example, a child may be carrying a label of being disruptive in class whenever the child argues with the class teacher (i.e. the meaning given to the child's behaviour in the classroom context for the speech act of saying something back to the teacher). The exchange of words between the child and the teacher builds up until the child is finally sent to the head teacher (the episode). As a result of this pattern the child starts to develop a generalized negative self-image (life script). This label of the child remains constant, as arguing with a teacher is seen as disruptive and disrespectful by the other teachers in this school and by people generally (cultural pattern). During one of these episodes the child becomes distressed and talks to the head teacher about a

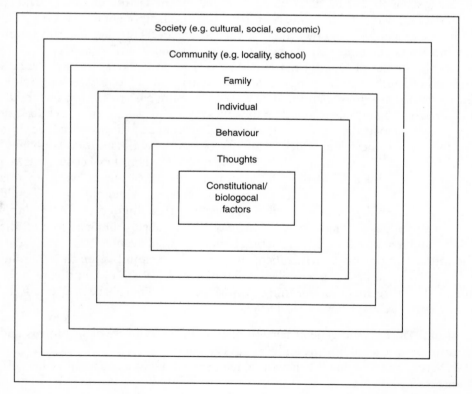

Figure 4.1. The child's levels of context

recent parental break-up. The head teacher offers the child some individual time to talk about the distress that has been caused by this breakdown in the parental relationship. The head teacher then starts to view the child's behaviour in the classroom as a result of the problems at home. The class teacher is also given this information which leads the teacher to interact with this child differently. The change in the meaning given to the child's behaviour therefore very quickly results in a different interactional pattern between the child and the class teacher, and leads to the child being able to settle down again in the classroom situation. Hence, while giving meaning to the child's behaviour in the classroom context gave one way of understanding the child's behaviour, it was not until the home context was understood that a new meaning was available for the same behaviour. Only when the child is understood across different contextual levels is it possible to think about interventions that will be of benefit to the child.

Understanding the child at different contextual levels

The following sections will discuss some of the different levels or contexts that are useful to think about when trying to understand a child's behaviour. These include the cultural context, the community context, the family context, the individual level, and the behavioural level. These are then followed by sections on formulating problems and the intervention strategies used in the systemic behavioural approach. Finally, a case example is given to illustrate the systemic behavioural approach that has been described.

The cultural level

The wider cultural context can have a major impact on the child's life. Global culturally accepted beliefs about children will influence how a child's behaviour is understood by the adults in the child's life. Some of these beliefs will be shared by all cultures, while some beliefs will be held by only some cultures. For example, some cultures place greater importance on individuation and independence of children, while other cultures place greater importance on family interdependency. Child-rearing practices and expectations placed on children can vary across different cultures, as well as across generations within the same culture. Such beliefs may lead to unrealistic expectations being placed on children by adults, or can equally lead professionals to pathologize behaviours which are culturally appropriate. Cultural beliefs are also influenced by the prevailing values and knowledge available through the media and health promotion initiatives (e.g. better to bottle-feed child versus breast-feeding, or the age at which a child should be started on solid foods).

The community level

The local community also have shared beliefs and interactional patterns which exert an influence on children's behaviour. Certain behaviours will be tolerated more in some communities than they will in others. The interaction between the cultural and community contexts can often place children in situations where they are caught between two different sets of expectations. For example, Western adolescents being seen to form relationships with others of the opposite sex can place adolescents from a more traditional cultural background in a conflict situation with their parents and their peer group when trying to form a close relationship. Alternatively, adolescents trying to form their homosexual identity within a peer group that places normative values on heterosexual relationships may experience conflicts about themselves and how they fit into their peer group. Expectations placed on children at school often vary from one school to another, and what may be seen as a problem in one school may not be seen as a problem in another; then the question becomes 'Is there a problem with the child's behaviour or is there a problem with how their behaviour is being seen by others, or does the problem actually lie at the contextual level?'

The family context

The family context is usually the level with which professionals become most directly involved when working in agencies that offer a service for children. The family context often provides a starting point in understanding a child's difficulties and is often the unit with which interventions are carried out. Further consideration of the child in the family context is given by Jackson and Sikara (1992). However, there has been a trend which has shifted from locating the problem within the individual to pathologizing the family. Such a view is unhelpful. It is more constructive to think about problems arising when families become stuck with a particular behavioural or interactional pattern which the professional may be able to help them deal with differently.

Family therapy models have described several aspects of the family context that are associated with children presenting with problems. The influence on children's behaviour of factors such as family structure, family hierarchies, roles within the family, family rules and interactional patterns has been acknowledged in structural family therapy (Minuchin, 1974; James and MacKinnon, 1986). This model views problem behaviours arising as a result of unclear family structure and family rules, members taking on inappropriate family roles, the presence of unhelpful interactional patterns between family members, and conflicts being channelled through a family member. A child is also thought to develop problems when placed in a conflict situation (e.g. school truancy being associated with a child being unable to express positive feelings to either parent when they are going through a divorce). Sometimes the reversal of family roles may lead to the child experiencing difficulties (e.g. the child developing headaches and starting to stay home more often after having to nurse a sick parent).

Sometimes the family's solutions to deal with a particular problem can become the problem, as these solutions and strategies no longer have the desired effect (de Shazer *et al.*, 1986; Cade, 1987). Solutions which are effective at one time may lose their effectiveness at other times, or are not appropriate when applied to every different problem. Also, it is important to note that while some strategies will work better with young children, other strategies may be more appropriate to use with older children. Sometimes a problem may only come into existence when the family have got caught up in unhelpful repeating interactional patterns and have lost their ability to find new ways of doing things. For example, keeping a child indoors for fighting with a sibling may work initially, but the impact of this strategy may be lost if the child is being kept indoors every evening while the siblings are able to go out to play. The unhelpful negative pattern may need to be broken in order to help the family find more positive ways of being together. Also, life-cycle changes often present the family with the challenge of finding new ways of doing things (e.g. a parent having to change the way he or she is with the children after the death of a spouse, or a couple having to find new ways of being 'a couple' after the birth of their first child). Problems may arise when life-cycle changes have not been negotiated successfully by the family.

Family beliefs can also play an important part in how children are able to function in their family, and how problems are defined. Systemic family therapy takes the view that problems arise when the beliefs no longer fit the behaviours that are occurring, or that the current beliefs have become outdated. Being able to find new beliefs and explanations can then lead to a diminishing of the problem (Mackinnon and James, 1987). For example, beliefs based on the deficits that a child with learning difficulties has will lower the expectations adults have of this child, whereas focusing on the child's assets may lead the adults to have more positive expectations of the child, giving the child a chance to live up to these.

The individual level

The child by interacting across the different levels above will be generating his or her own meaning about who he or she is. These meanings will be strongly influenced by those who are significant in the child's life. The resources that the child will have in being able to influence his or her own behaviour will depend on factors such as the child's age, level of physical and cognitive development, and other skills that he or she has acquired. On occasion working with the child individually in order to help him or her develop new behaviours can be very productive. At other times it may be more productive to help the adults change in the way they interact with the child, or to alleviate other family distress so that the adults are able to interact more positively with the child. The professional also needs to be able to understand child problems in relation to child development. Quite often adults can place unrealistic demands on a child which the child would not be able to meet given his or her physical, emotional or cognitive development. Also, normative information about children can be helpful to the professional in judging whether the problem with which the child has been labelled is actually age appropriate or whether it should constitute a real problem. Parental expectations of when children should be toilet-trained or at what age children should show fewer fears have to be judged against when such behaviours would actually be age appropriate. Such developmental issues are considered in further detail by Campbell (1990). While comparisons are useful it should also be kept in mind that children have their own individual characteristics and differences, and these will in turn determine what they do and how they are seen by others. It is important to keep the individual child in mind when thinking about all the factors that can influence his or her behaviour.

The behavioural level

Learning theory has developed a framework for understanding specific behaviours at the individual level. The traditional behavioural approach places particular emphasis on the objective observation of behaviour and hypothesis testing. In child work the most common units of behaviour observed include the frequency of the behaviour, its duration, its intensity, and the behaviour sequence as a whole (e.g. the number of temper tantrums that the child has per day, how severe they are, how long they last, or observation of the whole sequence associated with the temper tantrum). The child is usually observed directly, but similar information can be obtained by using rating scales or questionnaires. A more detailed account of the methods and principles underlying the observation of behaviour can be found in Ollendeck and Hersen (1984), McConaughy (1992), La Greca and Stone (1992) and Gelfand and Hartmann (1975).

Learning theory describes three main mechanisms by which new behaviours are thought to be learned namely classical conditioning, operant conditioning and observational learning. More recently the importance of cognitive processes associated with new learning has also been acknowledged. The classical conditioning paradigm states that a behaviour is established in response to specific triggers or stimuli. For example, a large dog (stimulus) running towards a child may lead to a fear response if this trigger is strong enough to have an impact on the child. The fear response may then become generalized to all dogs. If the child has had previous positive experiences with dogs then the above stimulus may not lead to a fear response. The operant conditioning paradigm states that behaviours are produced and maintained by the consequences following the behaviour (e.g. the dog biting the child may maintain the fear rather than the sight of the dog *per se*). Behaviours are also thought to be learnt by watching others (i.e. observational learning). For example, a fear of dogs may only be established in a child after the child has observed someone else showing a fear response to dogs. The child thinking about the dog may then lead to anticipatory anxiety about seeing a dog in the future, and it may be these thoughts that trigger or maintain the fear rather than the actual sighting of a dog. The application of learning theory to children's problems works on the premise of changing the triggers or the consequences in order to help the child learn new behaviour (see Herbert (1991 and 1987), Gelfand and Hartmann (1975), Graziano (1978), and Powers and Pickard (1992) for further details).

The single case experimental design provides a useful framework in which to evaluate the efficacy of the intervention (Barlow and Hersen, 1984). The most typical experimental design is that of collecting the baseline data, carrying out the intervention and then monitoring to see if there is any change as a result of the intervention (e.g. the baseline data shows that the child only does homework once a week; for the intervention the child is rewarded for doing homework; after 4 weeks the child is doing homework 5 times a week). Ethically it is usually not possible to withdraw the intervention in order to determine whether the change observed was due to the intervention or resulted from other factors. Some indication of this may be obtained when the intervention contingencies or rewards are gradually withdrawn in order for more naturally occurring contingencies to maintain the change.

While learning theory appears to be simple to understand and apply, there is a danger in applying this in a prescriptive manner. Without a proper formulation of the problem the intervention may be inappropriate and it may be rewarding the child for the wrong behaviours. The behavioural intervention strategies are open to misuse by both professionals and parents, and the behavioural approach has met with much criticism (e.g. time-out techniques, pin-down procedures for behaviour restraint). A behavioural approach can only work when it has the support of the child and his or her significant adults. The professional has to take account of the ethical issues to safeguard against the abuse of power over children.

A SYSTEMIC BEHAVIOURAL APPROACH

The traditional behavioural approach is limited without taking the wider context into account. Smail (1990) has argued a case for clinicians to take account of the wider context in their work.

A systemic behavioural approach involves helping a child and significant adults find alternative ways of interacting with each other. Quite often this involves helping them to find more positive interactional patterns, and pointing out to them the negative patterns in which they have become trapped. The most common complaints that adults have of children are that they are showing an unwanted behaviour too frequently (i.e. behaviour excess), or not showing a wanted behaviour often enough (i.e. behaviour deficit), or that they have not learnt a new behaviour yet (Herbert, 1987). In helping children and significant adults to acquire new ways of interacting together it is valuable to take a constructional approach (Zarkowska and Clements, 1988). This approach places the emphasis on looking at people's strengths and using these to build on, a view also shared by strategic family therapy (Cade 1987; de Shazer, 1986).

Any proposed change has to be negotiated and agreed by all the parties concerned. While a group of people may be able to change their interactional patterns towards each other, there may be times when a higher contextual factor may need to be addressed before other change is possible. The reasons why a particular problem has become a problem at a given point in time and an understanding about when would be the best time to tackle the problem are also important factors to determine. It is not uncommon to find that a particular behaviour has been occurring over a long period of time before it is brought to the attention of a professional. For example, a behavioural approach may seem appropriate for a child referred for a severe phobic reaction to loud noises. However, on further investigation it emerges that the parents of this child are locked in a losing battle to stop a neighbour making loud noises in the early hours of the night. The first time that the child had become fearful was after being startled from sleep by a loud drilling noise. The parents are desperate to move out of their council flat and are not very receptive to using a behavioural programme with their child. The difficulties with the neighbour are also starting to put a strain on their marital relationship. In this case it may be better to support the parents in getting a housing transfer to determine whether this will resolve the problem, and then to use the behavioural approach if the child's fear persists when they have moved house.

Formulating the problem

The systemic behavioural formulation has to take account of all of the contextual factors, individual factors, and factors associated with maintenance of the problem, that have already been described in the sections above. These factors then have to be connected in a way that provides a reasonable understanding of the presenting problem. The formulation provides the first step towards understanding the problem. However, the formulation should not be seen as the definitive version of what the truth is, but rather should act as the initial information which helps to develop other hypotheses as more information becomes available. A systemic behavioural formulation takes into account the recursive process (or two-way relationship) between the contextual factors and the specific behavioural sequences. This way of formulating children's behaviour is shown diagrammatically in Figure 4.2. The contextual factors and what is known about the individual factors can be thought of as providing the predisposing or setting conditions associated with the child's behaviour. The links between the triggering events, the actual behaviour observed, and the consequent responses can then be placed within the contextual framework in order to get an understanding of the functional value of the behaviour in question, and mechanisms by which this behaviour is maintained.

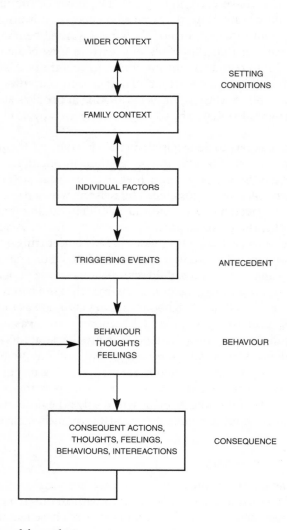

Figure 4.2. Behavioural formulation

Systemic behavioural interventions

The interventions are usually concerned with increasing a child's behaviour, decreasing it, or helping the child to develop new behaviours. Most of these interventions work at the level of changing the interactional patterns between children and significant adults, so that they are freed up to discover more positive ways of interacting with each other.

Increasing a child's behaviour

This can be done in several ways by changing the nature of the interaction between the child and the adults. The adults can be guided to respond more positively to targeted behaviours that they want to encourage in the child by carrying out rewarding actions towards the child when the desired behaviour occurs (e.g. give child praise, attention, affection, reward). It is then hoped that the new positive interactional patterns will themselves lead to further changes which act to maintain the desired behaviour in the child.

Helping the adults to understand the child's behaviour differently and then getting them to focus on the positive interactions can also have the desired effect. At times the existing positive interactions can be used as a way to link the targeted behaviour with those behaviours which occur more frequently. For example, a child's strength or interest can be used to help him or her learn new skills (e.g. helping the child learn maths by using play activities that the child does naturally and usually enjoys).

Contracts between older children and their parents can be negotiated so that all are clear about the rewards or sanctions that may follow the occurrence of the desired or undesired behaviour. Having a token system where the child has to earn the tokens for a targeted behaviour can be negotiated, so that the child is then able to trade the tokens in for a more tangible reward. The professional has to ensure that the contracts which are agreed between the child and the adults contain agreements that all of them will keep to. It is of no use having an agreement that one or both parties know that they will not be able to fulfil; it is often better to help people negotiate contracts that bind them to behaviours that are highly likely to be carried out. Once the more achievable changes are met then the more difficult behaviours can be negotiated through a contract. Also, safeguards have to be taken to ensure that the contract is not taking on a more sinister purpose by those agreeing to it (e.g. one party does not fulfil his or her part of the contract, or a failed contract being used by the adult to justify their case for no longer being able to care for the child).

Helping children acquire new skills

Selective interaction or cueing by the adult can be used to help shape the child's behaviour closer towards the desired behaviour. Parents are often doing this naturally without realizing it. For example, a young baby is given selective attention and spoken to by the parent when it makes any speech-like sound. Initially, the child may need encouragement in being able to achieve an approximation to the final skill that will be acquired (e.g. a baby given attention for being able to stand up with an adult's support, then being able to stand using other supports to be found around the home, to being able to stand without requiring any support).

The adults often model the desired behaviour and the child is able to learn by what has been observed. A lot of social behaviour can be thought of as being learnt in this way. The adults can also teach the child specific skills and behaviours, as a way of helping them acquire new skills (e.g. teaching a child to read, teaching him or her how to behave at a dinner party, teaching him or her how to ride a bicycle).

Decreasing unwanted behaviours

Helping the child give up certain behaviours can be done by the adult ignoring these, or modelling more appropriate behaviours for the child. The adult showing disapproval of the unwanted behaviour is another way most parents influence their child's behaviour.

Removing certain triggers or adult behaviours can also lead to a decrease in the child's behaviour (e.g. removal of bully from the class, parents learning not to shout too frequently when the child is being naughty).

Changing the way the child thinks about a particular trigger can also be an effective way to decrease behaviours. For example, helping the child to see that not all dogs are dangerous and getting the child to play with a friendly dog can help alleviate the child's fear about dogs. Also, helping the child develop specific skills such as relaxation techniques can help them reduce their fears.

The adult choosing to interact more positively to other behaviours of the child, instead of responding to those which are problematic to the adult, can lead to a new pattern of interactions such that the child gains more positive interactions for the other behaviours. The new gains may then make it easier for the child to lose the more negative behavioural patterns.

SUMMARY

The systemic behavioural approach uses the existing strengths of children and significant adults to channel their energies into more positive interactions in preference to the negative interactions that they have found themselves trapped in. This can be done by changing the focus away from the problem behaviour so that the positive interactions are given greater importance, or by making the helpful solutions more accessible to people, or by changing the beliefs that people have so that new beliefs can help them find different interactional patterns and ways of being together. To illustrate this approach a case example follows.

CASE EXAMPLE

The names of this family have been changed to ensure confidentiality. Joan, a 3-year-old girl was referred by a consultant paediatrician to the child mental health team because she was not eating. Joan had a twin sister, Jenny, and an older brother John aged six. Joan's father was 37 and her mother was 36. The twins were born six weeks before term and were cared for in the intensive care unit. The brother had also been a premature baby. When Joan was five months old she had suffered from whooping cough, and around this time the maternal grandmother had suffered a heart attack.

Following the heart attack the grandmother's eyesight had deteriorated and she had become housebound.

Joan's first year of life had been spent in and out of hospital, and at one point she had come close to death when her medical condition had worsened. In the nine months leading up to the referral she had enjoyed stable health. Since birth Joan had always been tube-fed. While Jenny had started to attend a day nursery, the nursery staff were only willing to take Joan when she no longer needed to be tube-fed. At the time of the referral Joan would touch certain foods and lick them on occasion (e.g. potato crisp), but she was not chewing or swallowing any food. Her brother had also had similar feeding problems, but these had been solved after the father had decided to force-feed him. For Joan this option seemed more difficult to apply as she was seen by her parents as a very fragile child. Both Joan and her sister were showing a developmental delay with Joan's being much greater than her sister's. The ongoing problems with Joan were adding to the marital tensions that seemed to have been there for some time. Joan's father did shift work and was usually not available at the times the appointments were made to see the family for home visits. What was notable was that the family were visited regularly by friends and the home care nursing staff from the hospital following up on Joan's medical care. Joan was observed to be over-friendly on the first occasion that she met the two new workers from the child mental health team.

A home visit was arranged to see Joan at dinner time. She was observed to play with food when sitting at the table with her siblings. The routine consisted of tube-feeding Joan at about 5 p.m. and then the family sitting down for their main meal about an hour later. Joan refused any attempts by her mother to feed her with solid foods by pushing her mother's arm away, having a temper tantrum or crying, at which point she would be left to play with the food on her plate. Joan generally managed to get a lot of attention for not eating.

The initial hypotheses generated about Joan's 'not eating' behaviour were:

- The early medical problems, developmental factors, and physiological factors had predisposed Joan to an eating problem. In developmental terms Joan had not acquired the skill of eating. Also, as she was tube-fed she had not yet learnt to associate hunger with eating behaviour.
- Family factors (e.g. grandmother's ill health, marital tensions) and family interactional patterns were also predisposing and maintaining factors of Joan's behaviour.
- Joan's early history had made her individuation more difficult as she was seen as a fragile child (e.g. she had nearly died around the time when the parents had made their only attempt to remove the tube and force-feed her).
- The tube-feeding had only become a more urgent problem at the point Joan should have started at a day nursery but was refused entrance until she was able to eat independently.

These hypotheses were used in the initial formulation about Joan's difficulties. This formulation is given in Figure 4.3.

The intervention focused initially on understanding why the parents had not been able to implement the sensible behavioural advice that they had already been given by the hospital medical staff (e.g. paediatric nurses, speech therapist). The issues identified in the formulation were discussed with the parents alone; in addition, they were asked to keep hospital appointments rather than being seen at home. Some of the discussions focused on the changes that could happen if Joan no longer had this problem, and some of the marital tensions were also addressed. It was hypothesized

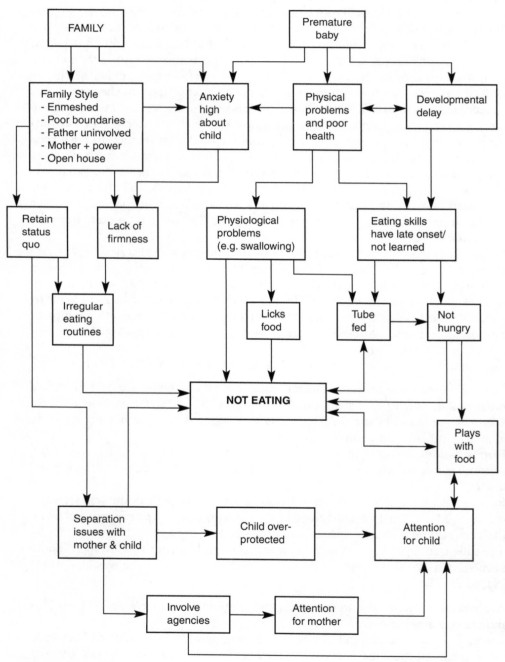

Figure 4.3. Clinical formulation

that unless the parents were able to agree on an approach to use with Joan and were both fully committed to this, any intervention suggested directly by the child mental health workers was unlikely to work. Each parent was thought to be negotiating a role within the marital relationship in a way that each of them was stuck in resolving unspoken power issues. Until this was done they could not work together in solving Joan's problem. Therefore, the parents were given a number of possible strategies to choose from, which they could use only if they had both agreed to it. The strategies suggested to them are given below.

Strategy 1

- Remove tube completely.
- Encourage Joan to eat baby food, solid food, Complan, and drink fluids.
- Give maximum attention to Joan when she eats any food.
- Minimize the attention that Joan gets for 'not eating' behaviour.
- Joan's weight should be regularly monitored by the home team paediatric nurse.
- Decide who would force-feed Joan if necessary.
- Parents to decide how long they would be willing to have Joan's tube removed, and under what circumstances they would have to put it back.

Strategy 2

- Change the time of the tube-feed to lunchtime only.
- Give maximum attention to Joan if she eats food during the evening meal.
- Give Joan minimum attention when she is tube-fed.
- If Joan creates a fuss during the evening meal send her to another room.
- If she has not eaten a specified amount of food in the evening then she is not given other snacks.
- Snacks given during the day should be removed if Joan is playing with them.

Strategy 3

- Gradually reduce the amount of tube-feed in amounts which are agreed before-hand.
- Give tube-feed at lunchtimes only.
- Give Joan minimum attention during the tube-feed.
- Give Joan maximum attention for eating food during the evening meal.
- Decide on which foods to get Joan to eat first (e.g. baby foods, solid foods).
- If a specified amount of food is not eaten in the evening then other snacks are not given later in the evening.
- If Joan refuses to eat or plays with food during the evening meal send her to another room.
- Snacks given during the day time should be taken away if Joan plays with them.

Strategy 4

- Do not try to change anything and continue to tube-feed Joan until such time that it is possible to try any of the strategies above.

The way that the intervention was negotiated with the parents took account of the factors that had been identified in the formulation. It was important that the parents were empowered to bring about the change, as well as the change being worthwhile for all concerned. For Joan the change meant entry to the day nursery. For her mother it could have meant that she had more time to develop her interests outside the home. For Joan's father bringing about the change meant that he was able to take the position of a successful man in this household. Joan's brother and sister could gain some of the attention and the mother's time that was currently being given to Joan. Also, the parents had to have a different belief about Joan in order for them to implement change: that Joan was healthy and strong enough to deal with not being tube-fed and that nothing terrible would happen if they took the tube out (i.e. she wouldn't die if they took the tube out). The parents were given the task of discussing together which of the strategies to use and to meet at the next appointment to go through how to implement their plan. For this appointment the parents proudly announced that they had taken the tube out a day after their last appointment and that it had been two weeks since she had last been tube-fed. At a one-month follow-up Joan was eating by herself, and four months later her mother had requested the ward staff not to tube-feed Joan when she had been admitted to the hospital following a chest infection.

The above case highlights how a systemic behavioural approach can provide a positive way of working with families and other child-adult systems. The behavioural technology without the systemic understanding can lead to the implementation of inappropriate interventions with children. Also, an understanding of the context and the meaning of the behaviour can act as a safeguard against the prescriptive manner in which traditional behavioural interventions have been made on occasion. Taking a wider perspective is in the best interests of the child, and would safeguard the child from abuse and inappropriate control in the name of therapy.

REFERENCES

Barlow, D. and Hersen, M. (1984) *Single Case Experimental Designs: Strategies for Studying Behaviour Change* (2nd edn). Oxford: Pergamon.

Cade, B. (1987) Brief/strategic approaches to therapy: a commentary. *Australian and New Zealand Journal of Family Therapy*, **8**, 1, 37–44.

Campbell, S. (1990) *Behaviour Problems in Pre-School Children: Clinical and Developmental Issues*. Hove: Guilford Press.

Crane, D. (1995) Introduction to behavioural family therapy for families with young children. *Journal of Family Therapy*, **17**, 229–42.

Cronen, V., Johnson, K. and Lannaman, J. (1982) Paradoxes, double binds and negative loops: an alternative theoretical perspective. *Family Process*, **21**, 91–112.

de Shazer, S., Berg, L., Lipchik, E., Nunnally, E., Molnar, A., Gingerich, W. and Weiner-Davis, W. (1986) Brief therapy: focused solution development. *Family*

Process, **25**, 207–21.

Gelfand, D. and Hartmann, D. (1975) *Child Behaviour: Analysis and Therapy*. Oxford: Pergamon.

Graziano, A. (1978) Behaviour therapy. In B. Wolman and J.R. Egan (eds) *A Handbook of Treatment of Mental Disorders in Childhood and Adolescence*. New York: Prentice-Hall, pp. 28–46.

Herbert, M. (1987) *Conduct Disorders of Childhood and Adolescence: A Social Learning Perspective* (2nd edn). New York: Wiley.

Herbert, M. (1991) *Clinical Child Psychology: Social Learning, Development, and Behaviour*. New York: Wiley.

Jackson, R. and Sikara, D. (1992) Child in the context of the family. In C.E. Walker and M.C. Roberts (eds), *Handbook of Clinical Child Psychology*. New York: Wiley Interscience, pp. 727–47.

James, K. and MacKinnon, K. (1986) Theory and practice of structural family therapy: illustration and critique. *Australian and New Zealand Journal of Family Therapy*, **7**, 4, 223–33.

La Greca, E. and Stone, W. (1992) Assessing children through interviews and behavioural assessments. In C.E. Walker and M.C. Roberts (eds) *Handbook of Child Clinical Psychology*. New York: Wiley Interscience, pp. 63–83.

McConaughy, S. (1992) Objective assessment of children's behavioural and emotional problems. In C.E. Walker and M.C. Roberts (eds) *Handbook of Child Clinical Psychology*. New York: Wiley Interscience, pp. 163–80.

MacKinnon, K. and James, K. (1987) The Milan systemic approach: theory and practice. *Australian and New Zealand Journal of Family Therapy*, **8**, 2, 89–98.

Minuchin, S. (1974) *Families and Family Therapy*. Cambridge, MA: Harvard University Press.

Ollendeck, T. and Hersen, M. (1984) *Child Behaviour Assessment Principles and Procedures*. Oxford: Pergamon.

Powers, S. and Pickard, H. (1992) Behaviour therapy with children. In E.C. Walker and M.C. Roberts (eds) *Handbook of Child Clinical Psychology*. New York: Wiley Interscience, pp. 749–63.

Smail, D. (1990) Design for a post-behaviourist clinical psychology. *Clinical Psychology Forum*, August, 2–10.

White, M. (1989) *Selected Papers*. Adelaide: Dulwich Centre Publications.

Zarkowska, E. and Clements, J. (1988) *Problem Behaviours in People with Learning Difficulties: A Practical Guide to a Constructional Approach*. London: Croom Helm.

CHAPTER 5

The Psychodynamic Approach to Children with Problems

Francis Dale

INTRODUCTION

I would like to begin by defining, for the purposes of this chapter, how I will be using the term 'psychodynamic'. *Psyche* – soul, spirit, mind – derives from the Greek word *psukhe* which means breath, life, soul. *Dynamic* refers to a force or power which is in motion or active in an operational sense. It is clear therefore, that the psychodynamic approach refers to that body of science which seeks to study the interrelationship between observed behaviour and the psychic forces underlying it. Although the existence of psychic forces – the unconscious and unconsciously motivated behaviour – has long been accepted, their aetiology, the role they play in mental and emotional disturbance, and their use in therapeutic interventions have not. In the following, I will be looking at the kinds of situation in which the psychodynamic approach is useful, both as a tool for thinking about the presenting problem, and as a therapeutic intervention.

THE PRESENTING PROBLEM

This refers to the problem for which the child was referred for help. As children can present with so many different problems and symptoms, it will be useful if we attempt to categorize them.

- *Delinquency/behavioural problems*
  Problems in this category relate to all kinds of antisocial behaviour where destructive and aggressive behaviour is mainly directed towards other people and/or their property.
- *Aberrant behaviour*
  Any behaviour which is a cause for concern and which significantly deviates from what would be expected in a given situation can be an indication that something is troubling the child.

c *Emotional disturbance*
  Depression, excessive anxiety, sleep disorder, and becoming easily upset (overly emotional) can be noted in the child.
c *Psychosis*
  Bizarre, delusional behaviour (infantile and adolescent schizophrenia), extreme withdrawal and avoidance of contact with others (e.g. autism) fall into this category.
c *Eating disorders*
  These include failure to thrive, anorexia nervosa, bulimia.
c *Psychosomatic disorders*
  Asthma, eczema, soiling, and bed-wetting are in this grouping.
c *Self-harm*
  The child puts him or herself at risk from injury, or makes deliberate attacks on his or her person, through either physical mutilation or the ingestion of harmful substances.
c *Compulsive or obsessional behaviour*
  There is an infinite variety of obsessional/compulsive behaviour patterns and so the following are merely indicative of the range and complexity of symptoms one may come across: head-banging, thumb-sucking (excessive or age inappropriate), excessive masturbation, over-eating, rocking, obsessive tidying or washing of hands, compulsive checking that windows or doors are shut, and so on.

In looking at the above list (which is by no means exhaustive) one might be forgiven for wondering where to start or how to find a systematic comprehensive or coherent therapeutic model for understanding – let alone treating – such diverse problems and symptomatology. A partial solution is offered through the unique understanding with which psychoanalysis approaches and tries to unravel the meaning and function of human behaviour. The psychodynamic model makes certain assumptions regarding all behaviour – whether healthy or pathological – which allow us to look behind the symptom, or behaviour causing concern, to the underlying dynamic forces and defences which are motivating the individual.

The first, and arguably the most important of these assumptions, is *psychic determinism*. This notion is based on the most crucial, far-reaching and powerful assertion – originally made by Freud – regarding the existence and *function* of unconscious processes. I have stressed the word 'function' because the existence of unconscious thought processes is no longer controversial. What is controversial is *how* these forces operate and how we are to understand them.

The second assumption, is that all behaviour – whether physical or mental – is at some level metaphoric or symbolic. In other words, alongside and in parallel with every piece of conscious behaviour, and the meaning attributed to it, there exists an unconscious 'shadow' which is capable of adding another dimension, a deeper meaning and significance to our surface (that is, conscious) understanding.

From this, follows a third assumption – that all psychic events are overdetermined. To quote from Rycroft: 'A symptom, dream-image, or any other item of behaviour is said to be overdetermined if it has more than one meaning or expresses drives and conflicts derived from more than one level or aspect of the personality . . .' (Rycroft, 1972).

These basic assumptions allow us to attribute different levels of meaning to the behaviour of children with psychological and emotional problems; but, more importantly, they provide us with a conceptual framework within which hypotheses can be formulated, tested and then shaped into therapeutic interventions.

THERAPEUTIC INTERVENTIONS

These can and, I would argue, should be based on an overall understanding not just of the symptom – the pathological aspect of behaviour in question – but on the individual, the family, the social and cultural context, and the consequences that the problem which brought the child into treatment has had on the system as a whole.

This last notion derives from cybernetics and the systemic view which holds that one can only fully understand the individual – and his or her particular symptomatology – by taking into account the complex and highly interdependent family and social relationships which comprise the child's significant attachments.

This more macroscopic view helps us to understand the external influences exerted on the child and to estimate their impact on his or her behaviour. It also alerts us to the importance of taking the overall pattern of the child's relationships (past and present) into account, while attempting to engage actively with, and seek the support of, the parents and wider supportive network available to the child.

We can see from the foregoing that any intervention should, ideally, not only take account of the dynamic interplay between conscious and unconscious forces operating in the individual child but also of the wider influences from family, friends and the environment.

While of course, in practice, one rarely treats either the individual or the family system of which he or she is a part as unrelated entities, in terms of formulating hypotheses it is important to be able to differentiate between them conceptually – certainly during the initial assessment and during the process of formulating a tentative diagnosis. (Sometimes one can arrive at very firm and reliable diagnoses early on in assessment, but I have used the word 'tentative' because, in general, it is always wise to err on the side of caution, particularly so as not to close down one's thinking too early and so exclude other alternative diagnoses.)

Assessment and diagnosis

It is very important to remember when making a diagnosis that one does not try to engage the child in therapy. There may be 'therapeutic benefits' to a diagnostic interview or assessment, but the *primary* aim is not therapeutic. It is to get information in order to gain sufficient understanding of a problem or symptom so that a decision can be made on an appropriate treatment regime which may well not be psychodynamic. Different symptoms respond in different ways to different kinds of intervention. This means the therapist should have at least a basic grounding in and familiarity with other major treatment models, particularly the systemic and family therapy, and cognitive, behavioural models.

Formulating hypotheses

In part, because human behaviour is so over-determined and because of the impossibility of examining real and meaningful human interactions in controlled laboratory conditions, psychoanalytic theories and therapeutic interventions can never attain the rigour of proof of the natural sciences. In addition, many of the most profound insights into the human predicament have, and still do, come from intuition – which is by definition a highly subjective process. However, science and intuition are not necessarily incompatible. It is the manner in which we test our intuitions that decides whether we are using scientific methodology or not.

GATHERING INFORMATION

In the initial phase of gathering information, the analytically orientated therapist will tend to be more active, gently trying to explore with the child (and parent who is usually present for at least part of the first session) what the child's ideas and fantasies are with regard to coming to see the therapist. I believe it is important for both the parents and the child to hear early on what each has to say about the problems which have led them to refer the child for help. I have often found that a child has no idea why he or she has been brought to see me, or if he or she has been told, it has not been explained in terms he or she could understand. (Even when it has been properly explained, sometimes the child *does not want to hear* and blocks it out.)

Encouraging the family to confront the issue openly can also be the first step in lessening denial and in empowering the parents. Part of the problem may be the parents' reluctance to 'own' or accept responsibility for what is happening. In this case, the therapist has to be careful not to let the parent(s) 'offload' the problem, the responsibility for it and any possible resolutions regarding it, on to the therapist. Once this happens, any failure in the treatment will be blamed on the therapist and the chance of engaging the parent(s) in a cooperative way will be lost.

Once the presenting problem has been identified, this can become the focus for a series of questions aimed at identifying the function of the problem – for both the child and the family.

The 'function' of the symptom

There are two ways of looking at problem behaviour or symptoms. At one end, the therapeutic intervention consists in attempting to suppress or get rid of the presenting problem: an aspirin for a headache, positive re-enforcement (star chart) or bell-pad for enuresis, tranquillizers for anxiety and so on. At the other, the symptom or presenting problem is seen as a 'sign' or metaphor which points to an underlying problem which cannot be expressed in any other way. From the psychodynamic perspective therefore, symptom relief, although not ignored, is frequently not the main focus of the intervention.

The notion that symptoms – or any behavioural abnormality – can be seen in functional terms is a very powerful one. It allows us to ask questions and formulate hypotheses which might not have otherwise seemed pertinent to the issue at hand.

Before going on to give some clinical examples of the psychodynamic approach to children's problems, I want to say something about the kinds of questions which are useful both in gathering information and in formulating hypotheses.

Asking the 'right' questions

First of all, from a *systemic* perspective, you need to ask the question 'Why now?' That is, what is the significance of the timing of a) the child's problem, or b) if the problem is not recent, why are the parents referring the child for help now? Secondly, in exploring the *function* of the symptom, not just for the child, but for the family as a whole, you need to know who is most concerned. It is also useful to know how the problem is affecting the family. It may be that they are not concerned but the school is. If it is impacting on the family, what is happening because of the child's problem that would not otherwise be happening? In other words, how is the problem 'mobilizing' the family? Exploring the answers to questions of this kind should eventually reveal to you the dynamic meaning of the child's problems and how they interact with the family dynamics.

We now come to the much more difficult question of how to find out from the child – who may not trust you, have any idea about what is troubling him or her or, if he or she does, how to express it in words – the most effective way to help him or her. This brings us to an examination of the most crucial aspect of work with children – the therapeutic relationship.

THE THERAPEUTIC RELATIONSHIP

There are important differences between working with adults and working with children. Children are not just 'little adults'. Children think differently, they experience the world differently, they react differently and they respond to stress, uncertainty and trauma in a much more intense, undiluted and subjective way than adults do. The younger the child, the greater will the disparity be between adult (mature) coping and more primitive (immature) ways of coping. Without doubt, the most significant difference is in the way children communicate.

Whereas adults almost invariably use words and concepts in order to communicate about their thoughts and feelings, children use play and the interaction between themselves and the therapist as the primary means of communication.

Communicating through play

Although it would be an overgeneralisation to say that children play in order to communicate, there is no question that children *do* convey through their play their ongoing concerns and preoccupations. You could even say that the 'natural language' of childhood is play and that play is the 'Royal Road' to the child's unconscious processes as Freud believed dreams were in the case of adults. This knowledge provides those who work with children an ideal vehicle through which non-verbal communication can occur. (Dale, 1992)

Directive versus non-directive play

In general, I try to be as non-directive as possible with children I see in therapy. There are several reasons for this.

First, we all have our own preconceived ideas, personal biases and belief systems. Even when we try to be aware of them, they can still subtly affect our ability to be impartial and objective. The more we direct a child in therapy, the greater the risk that we impose *our* agenda on to the child and cease to be receptive and open to his or her attempts to communicate.

Secondly, if you become too active and directive, you will cease being an observer and lose your neutral stance. Once this happens, you risk entering into an unconscious collusion with the part of the child that may be heavily defended against being understood.

Finally, you need to respect the child's right to find his or her own way of entering into a therapeutic relationship with you, at a pace and speed which he or she can manage.

Perhaps the most important skill in any therapist is the capacity to listen. If you are making too much 'noise' yourself, you won't be able to listen to the child, and he or she won't have the experience of being listened to and 'heard' properly.

I would now like to give an account of the assessment of a nine-year-old boy who was referred to me following his reception into care. I hope this will illustrate some of the above themes, especially the importance of play in non-verbal communication.

'HOLDING MUMMY TOGETHER'

Background

The mother of Paul (not his real name) was a chronic schizophrenic who lived alone with Paul in a council flat on a very run-down housing estate. Paul had never had any contact with his father who had left soon after he was born. Prior to the referral, Paul's mother had withdrawn from any social contact and become a virtual recluse. As a result of school non-attendance, a home visit was made. All the doors and windows were barricaded and the police had to break down the front door. Paul was found to be severely underweight, living in appalling conditions and feeding off whatever he could find in the flat. His mother was sectioned and Paul taken into care.

Therapeutic contact: first session

When I went to collect Paul he came with me very easily, showing no obvious anxiety. He seemed very interested in all of the things in the room and walked around it pulling on the cupboard doors, looking into the sand tray and at the box on the table which contained his play material.

When I said that this was his box to use while I was seeing him, he expressed surprise and also pleasure and opened up the box. He immediately began to play with a rubbish truck, turning a handle which operated the press inside the truck to push the rubbish out.

He spent the rest of the session exploring themes about being stuck, and having to seal off cracks or holes in the things he was playing with so that nothing could spill out. His anxiety concerned dirt and mess spilling out everywhere. For example, he blocked up all the doors and windows of a toy house with bricks until every gap was completely sealed.

Interpretation (hereafter shown in italics) *I commented that I thought he was telling me something about being shut up or sealed in; about things needing to be blocked off so that whatever was inside couldn't get out. Perhaps Paul thought that what was inside was dangerous, dirty or messy, and that was why it had to be sealed in. Perhaps he was also wondering if there was a space here where it might be safe to look at these dangerous and messy feelings that were shut inside and was wanting to know what sort of a 'dust lorry' I was and whether I could hold on to all the mess inside – his mess – or whether I would just push it all out again and not take care of it for him.*

> **Internal commentary** It would seem that, through his play, Paul was exploring with me the possibility that the dangerous thoughts and feelings which he feared might spill out in an uncontained, damaging and destructive way, could be put into words, or thought about, so that they would not become too frightening and unmanageable.

Paul then used a dumper truck to remove wet sand from one end of a sand tray to pile it at the opposite end creating a large space which was clear of sand.

I suggested that he was wanting to find a safe place where the messy and confused feelings inside of him could be taken care of.

He then picked up the dumper truck and shook it trying to turn the wheels around in the palm of his other hand, saying they had become stuck.

Here I wondered if he thought that I would get stuck or bogged down if I tried to help him to sort out the mess and he might then feel that he had damaged me in some way with his mess.

As he carried on playing Paul revealed more clearly the nature of some of his underlying anxieties. He had shaped the sand into a mountain. As he tried to make a crater in the top part, the sand began to crack around the edges and started sliding down. He commented 'It's falling apart, it's collapsing.'

I pointed out that a mountain was something which should be firm and strong, but this one seemed to be falling apart, breaking into pieces.

Paul then began to shore the sides up with his hands.

*I said that he felt that **he** had to hold it together, to prevent it from falling apart.*

Paul then made a hole or crater in the top with his finger. It again cracked apart at the top. Paul shored it up again.

I suggested to Paul that this was his way of telling me about a mummy who was in a mess, like this rock or mountain which should be strong but which was cracking and falling apart.

Paul then made a deep hole in the sand, like a large crater. The sides collapsed and fell apart. He then repeatedly crashed a sports car and a police car into the sides of the mountain.

I commented that it looked as if they [the cars] were angry with the collapsed mountain – as if they were trying to get inside but kept being pushed away.

Paul: 'They want a cave.'

I felt that he was telling me that they were looking for somewhere safe, a place they could get right inside of and be protected.

Internal commentary In his play with the sand I thought Paul was really telling me something about how he experienced his mother at an unconscious level. He feels that he has to protect her because she is collapsing and falling apart, when in reality *she* should be protecting *him* and providing him with a safe place.

This situation has made him angry, but he then experiences his anger as frightening and dangerous because his mother is so vulnerable and collapsing. I think this puts Paul in a very difficult dilemma: on the one hand of needing to look after and protect his vulnerable mother; on the other, of feeling there is no one to look after him and nowhere he can put his anger and frustration at this mother who is not looking after him in the way in which he needs her to.

I felt that Paul confirmed these ideas when, towards the end of the session, he put a male and female figure from his box into the sand and repeatedly made them fight and make up. In this piece of play I think he is showing his ambivalence regarding his angry feelings: he wants to fight her, to punish her, to tell her off but at the same time, he needs to keep things good between his mother and himself.

Paul said, 'They're fighting!' and proceeded to bury them both up to their necks in the sand.

I said to Paul that he seemed to be anxious about fighting and angry feelings which he wanted to bury in the sand where no one could see them.

In response to this interpretation, Paul placed a white curtain hook into the sand by the two figures and said, 'It's a light!'

I suggested that he was telling me two things: first, that he was frightened of this collapsing mummy breast (the mounds of sand he had made were very breast-like in shape) *as well as the angry feelings which he wanted to bury; but also, that he was wanting to put a light there which meant that another part of him wished that we could find our way to these buried feelings and deal with them.*

Destruction, chaos and mess: remaining sessions

The themes which had emerged in the first session continued throughout the remaining three sessions. He returned again and again to the themes of anxiety, of there being too many powerful and destructive feelings inside for him to be able to deal with them, and of his fear that if these feelings did get out they would overwhelm him. He also showed me quite clearly that he did not think that anybody else could deal with the overwhelming mess he felt he had inside.

In one session, he asked if he could pour water into the sand. He then made a small crater in the sand into which he poured some water and watched as the water slowly drained away. He then said excitedly, 'It's all gone!' and poured more water into the crater until the sides started to cave in. He became agitated saying, 'It's going over the top!'

I made a connection between the water flooding over the top of the crater and the mess inside of him which kept threatening to spill out and leave him all leaky and collapsing.

He then put a car into the water: 'Look! it's sinking, it's going under!'

I suggested that perhaps he thought that I might be like the car – that if I tried to help him with the mess I might become overwhelmed and made useless by it. If this happened, he might become anxious and feel that he had put the mess into me and destroyed me (as perhaps in unconscious phantasy he felt he had destroyed his mother).

He then made a barrier across the width of the sand tray by piling the sand up in a ridge and pouring more and more water into one end until it started to leak past the barrier, spilling over the top until it collapsed.

I said that he was showing me that he felt the mess that he had inside (i.e. the angry destructive feelings, the confusion and anxiety, etc.) *were so powerful that he needed some way of protecting himself from them so that they did not spill out and spoil everything. He felt that he couldn't manage on his own because the mess always leaked out and overwhelmed his defences.*

Paul then put three cars he had been playing with on separate mounds of sand raised above the water and therefore above the mess which was in the rest of the tray.

I said that I felt that he was needing to have a place where he wouldn't become overwhelmed by all the mess that was inside.

In response to this, Paul gathered the sand together with his hands to create a large mound of wet sand in the middle of the tray saying, 'We won't tell anyone who made this mess, will we?'

I commented that Paul felt guilty about the mess that he had made and was anxious that it was destructive and dangerous and wanted me to reassure him that I wouldn't tell him off or punish him because of it.

Paul confirmed his anxiety about the mess he had inside and the damage it might do to others when, at the end of the session, he took the three cars which he had buried in the sand, washed them in the sink and carefully dried them before putting them back in his toy box. On leaving the room, Paul showed in a very concrete and physical way his need to have a place to put his internal mess by going to the toilet and doing a very large pooh.

In the final session with me, Paul returned to the theme of having a collapsed mother whom he feels he has to look after and take responsibility for. He showed this by making a construction from bricks in the sand which he then said were some blocks of flats. I reminded him that he used to live in a block of flats with his mother. Paul nodded and said that they lived on the sixth floor. He then added a bridge between two of the blocks of flats.

I wondered if he was trying to make a link or bridge between me and his mother as if he wanted us to be connected in some way. Perhaps he was needing a space here to think about his relationship with his mother.

Following this, Paul began to undermine the wooden pillars supporting the blocks of flats by crashing a car into them.

I pointed out that he seemed to feel that it was his fault that everything had collapsed.

For the first time since I had been seeing Paul, he openly showed his distress. He overturned a wooden house and began to fill it with sand.

I commented that he seemed to feel that there was just too much mess for him to cope with.

At the end of this session – which was the final meeting – Paul took all the cars and washed them carefully and then wanted to throw them into his toy box from the other side of the room.

I said to Paul that I thought he was angry with me and that he was showing me by throwing the cars into the box, that he felt I was 'throwing' him away and rejecting him.

Diagnostic formulation

The main theme which ran through all of my sessions with Paul related to his fear of being overwhelmed by the intensity of the feelings he experiences inside himself. These feelings are a combination of anger, despair, destructiveness and a belief that nobody can help him deal with them. In this phantasy, Paul may feel that his anger – although not expressed verbally – was responsible for both his mother's collapse and his being removed from home. As a result of his mother's failure to recognize, contain and manage his difficult-to-bear thoughts and feelings, Paul feels that he has to protect other people from how he feels inside.

In relation to this, I think it would be very important for Paul to develop a trusting relationship with an adult who could show him that he or she could survive Paul's anger and be able to help him deal with the unresolved feelings he has inside. Associated with the above is Paul's fear of being dirty or bad inside. Again, a trusting relationship with an adult might help him to feel less anxious that he is wholly bad inside.

In his relationship with me, Paul revealed a strong need to protect me from the mess, badness, anger and rage that he feels he has inside. This is, I think, an indication of the way he feels about his mother. He feels he needs to protect her from his anger, to look after her and to care for her. In this sense, he is a 'parentified child', and as such I think he has had to deny his own needs: to be cared for and protected, in order to look after a very vulnerable and unstable parent.

In spite of his belief that he has something frightening and dangerous inside, Paul was able, through his play, to communicate his fears and anxieties in a way which showed he was available and ready to be helped and has sufficient motivation and ego strength to make good use of therapy.

I have gone through Paul's sessions in some detail in order to show the interaction between his non-verbal behaviour (his play) and his unconscious preoccupations. In psychodynamic therapy this linkage between conscious and unconscious processes comes about through the use of interpretations.

INTERPRETATION: THE AGENT OF CHANGE

Interpretation is the *sine qua non* of analytic psychotherapy. It is the means by which the unknown can become known, resistances and defences overcome, and the agent by way of which real change can occur. As such, it is a very powerful therapeutic tool which requires a precise understanding of what it can and cannot do, and when it can and cannot be used.

First and foremost, an interpretation should be a considered response to something the child is telling the therapist he or she wants help with now. It should never be used as a means for the therapist to use therapeutic insight in order to give the child information which he or she is not yet ready to receive. ... This means that the 'timing' of interpretations is an important factor in deciding how they will be received by the patient and in his or her capacity to make use of them.

But what exactly is an 'interpretation' in the psychoanalytic sense of the word? It is not merely commenting on what a patient is saying or doing and neither is it giving him or her 'information'. It is a way of giving structure, meaning and purpose to sometimes apparently meaningless and unconnected utterances. As such, it is a technique or model for thinking about language (and non-verbal behaviour) at a meta level. In making interpretations, the therapist is generating hypotheses based on his or her understanding of the symbolic content of the child's communications. This means that in order to formulate an interpretation the therapist has to restructure his or her thinking from operating solely on a linear, logical, deductive model, to one which can operate on two levels at the same time: one which can cope with analysing meaning at a literal causal level, while at the same time addressing meaning at a metaphorical level. The following examples should illustrate how an interpretation is both a clinical technique for interacting with the patient's unconscious as well as a way of thinking symbolically.

Early on in therapy with me an adolescent boy produced the following dream:

On the way to his session with me he saw a large brass telescope in the window of an antique shop. It could magnify 10 times and he thought it was really good but unfortunately it was attached to an ornate chair and he did not think he would be able to use it outside to see the stars. He could not make up his mind between the telescope, which cost £37.00 and membership of his father's golf club which was £25.00. He thought that if it was not attached to the chair it would be cheaper as the chair probably put the price up. The woman in the shop said it was a valuable instrument and well worth the price he would have to pay. He then noticed that the telescope had gold bits on it.

The only association he had to the dream was seeing a telescope in one of the windows of the clinic where I saw him. It seems that the telescope is linked to my ability to observe and to focus on distant events. The fact that it was prominently displayed in the antique shop and made of precious metal suggested that it was both a valuable asset as well as being an instrument with which one could look into the past in order to see things in close-up. It was also an admission from my patient that he needed help in seeing things in this way and could not do it without the telescope. The ornate chair seemed to be linked to my chair and to his desire for my telescope – that is, my ability to see inside him – but without having to be tied to me. Wanting to take it outside represented his urge to 'steal' my 'instrument' as well as his envy of it. The price for the telescope probably related to how much value he placed on me and my abilities as a 'valuable instrument' as opposed to joining the golf club which was a denial of his status as a patient and which gave him membership of 'my' club and equal status with me.

In the above example, one can see how the same quality – analytical insight – is both admired and envied, wanted and feared, and how important it is in interpreting this kind of symbolic material to pay attention to these different levels of meaning. There was also another level of meaning to this dream which related to this boy's anxiety about my potency. The wish to possess for himself the valuable telescope also stood for his desire to be more potent than me, but also stirred up his anxiety about my using it (as a symbolic penis) to get inside him.

The second example concerns an 8-year-old girl who had been in therapy with me at the time of my daughter's birth, as a result of which she missed two of her therapy sessions. The anniversary of my daughter's birth coincided with Easter and my patient wanted to make an Easter card for me to give to her. (It is accepted practice in psychoanalytic psychotherapy not to reveal details of one's private life. However, this patient gained the information from another source.) She seemed to have great difficulty in getting the card the way she wanted it, but at the third attempt she got it right and handed it to me. In the middle of the card she had painted an Easter egg above which she had written 'Happy Eatser'. I made a connection between eggs and babies and chocolate and pooh and said that although she thought she wanted to give my daughter a present, her true feelings towards her were revealed by her misspelling Easter on her third attempt to turn it into a word which had a very different meaning – Eats(h)her. What she was really showing me was how angry she was with my daughter and how she wanted not to feed her but to poison her, to fill her up with pooh and to turn her into a 'shit' baby. On hearing this interpretation, my patient gave vent to a prolonged burst of laughter saying: 'Yes, she is a shit baby! It was meant!'

Here we can see that the act of interpreting the underlying symbolic content of this material made it possible for this girl to own her destructive and aggressive feelings which otherwise might have been experienced as unacceptable. If her disguised attack on me had not been interpreted, she may have experienced some relief but at the same time would have been anxious at my inability to protect her positive feelings for me from her envious attacks. The interpretation, then, had both a cathartic effect of releasing hidden aggression but had also reassured her that her aggressive phantasies could be contained and thought about (Dale, 1990).

APPLICATIONS OF THE PSYCHODYNAMIC APPROACH

As I mentioned earlier, in thinking about the kinds of situation in which the psychodynamic approach would be useful, it is important to differentiate between psychoanalysis as a method for *thinking about meaning*, and as the chosen mode of therapeutic intervention.

Thinking about meaning

Whatever treatment choice we decide on, whether systemic, behavioural, cognitive or psychodynamic, the more comprehensive our understanding is of both conscious and unconscious factors in determining our patients' pathology, the more effective will be our therapeutic interventions. In this sense, the psychodynamic model can be a valuable diagnostic tool, *regardless* of the treatment option we may eventually decide on.

Psychodynamic therapy as the treatment choice

As has already been implied, some problems respond better and more readily to other kinds of therapeutic intervention. If we take the first category, *delinquency/ behavioural problems*, these are often more successfully managed employing behavioural methods (using positive or negative reinforcement procedures) or group therapy (which can be psychodynamic) or in extreme cases, in residential institutional settings which provide the boundaries, discipline and containment which severely acting out children need.

In the fifth category, eating disorders, frequently a combination of family therapy, group work, behavioural and cognitive therapy and psychodynamic interventions succeed where one approach on its own would fail to address all of the issues involved.

Children who self-harm may also need to be in an institutional setting – possibly with their moods stabilized by tranquillizers or anti-depressants before they can be reached by a more interpretive approach.

Finally, compulsive, obsessional behaviour, although it can be treated successfully using the psychodynamic approach, often responds favourably to a combination of behavioural/cognitive therapy.

ACKNOWLEDGEMENT

The author gratefully acknowledges the kind permission of Routledge Publishers to quote from his chapter in *The Management of Children with Problems,* edited by V.P. Varma (London, 1990).

REFERENCES

Dale, F.M.J. (1990) The psychoanalytic psychotherapy of children with emotional and behavioural difficulties. In V.P. Varma (ed.) *The Management of Children with Emotional and Behavioural Difficulties*. London: Routledge.

Dale, F.M.J. (1992) The art of communicating with vulnerable children. In V.P. Varma (ed.) *The Secret Life of Vulnerable Children*. London: Routledge.

Rycroft, C. (1972) *A Critical Dictionary of Psychoanalysis*. London: Penguin.

CHAPTER 6

The Management of Children with Problems in Mainstream and Special Schools

Colin J. Smith

Within an educational context, discussing children with problems might cover a very broad canvas, from pupils who are merely naughty or nervous, but who nonetheless present problems for some teachers, to young people who are psychotic or seriously disturbed, who present problems for themselves and all who care for them. For the purposes of the present discussion, the focus will be on that part of the continuum which covers what are sometimes described as disruptive or disaffected pupils in mainstream schools to those with more serious problems, who though not mentally ill in medical terms do have special educational needs, which may require provision outside the mainstream in special schools or units, at least for a period of time. Decisions about helping these children depend very much on how effectively schools have developed their policies for behaviour management and for meeting special educational needs.

RECENT ADVICE ON PUPILS WITH PROBLEMS

Following the Education Act 1993, a Code of Practice on the Identification and Assessment of Children with Special Educational Needs has been established. This involves a series of school-based stages of assessment, requiring a record to show that intervention has been attempted at Stage 1 by classroom and subject teachers; at Stage 2 by more detailed individual educational plans, devised and reviewed with the help of the school's Special Educational Needs Co-ordinator (SENCO); and at Stage 3 by the involvement of external specialist advice from educational psychologists or local authority advisory and support services.

Only in very exceptional circumstances will there be a move to a statutory assessment of whether the provision of a statement of special educational needs is required, unless these stages have been completed. Even on completion of a state-ment, there will be a presumption that any additional provision for the child with special educational needs will be in the mainstream school, if at all possible. At the same time, since this policy emphasizes 'inclusive' education, there has been a rapid growth in the number of pupils excluded from schools because of behaviour problems. It does appear that where special educational needs involve emotional and behavioural difficulties, schools find it hard to balance the individual's need for support with the institution's need to maintain an orderly environment.

In addressing this issue, the Department for Education has produced a package of advice entitled *Pupils With Problems* (DFE, 1994). This consists of a collection of circulars providing guidance on a range of issues, including provision for the education of sick children (DFE, 12/94) and children being looked after by local authorities (DFE, 13/94). However, most relevant to the management of pupils with problems are the circulars DFE, 8/94 which offers guidance on pupil behaviour and discipline; DFE, 9/94 which is about the education of children with emotional and behavioural difficulties; DFE, 10/94 on exclusions from school; and DFE, 11/94 concerning the education of children otherwise than at school.

Taken together, these circulars reflect an official response to children, whose behaviour challenges conventional systems for maintaining good discipline and providing pastoral care in mainstream and special schools. The circulars, which were produced after extensive consultation with local education authorities and schools, aim to provide a synthesis of good practice in mainstream and special schools. Their emphasis is upon maintaining pupils with problems within the mainstream as far as possible, ensuring that, where necessary, suitable education is available for them outside the mainstream, whether in special schools or other forms of provision and working towards as speedy as possible a return for them to the mainstream, wherever that is practicable.

How can the helpful general guidance on whole-school policies contained in this package be best applied in practice in mainstream and special schools? In responding to this question, a conceptual framework is provided by what have been described as the four 'Ms' of teaching: Management, Mediation, Modification and Monitoring (Smith, 1991; Smith and Laslett, 1993). Although these four aspects of teaching overlap, they can be seen as each relating primarily to particular aspects of school life for pupils with problems. Viewing the official advice in *Pupils With Problems* in this way raises a number of questions about the application of these guidelines in relation to particular aspects of school organization.

MANAGEMENT AND THE CURRICULUM

Management refers to skill in the organization and presentation of lessons in such a way that all pupils are actively engaged in learning. This refers to aspects of classroom management, analysing the different elements and phases of a lesson, to selecting appropriate material and methods for teaching and to reducing sources of friction in the classroom. Management is concerned with the curriculum and the continuum of provision for pupils with problems. Can their needs be met in the mainstream with support, given additional help to cope with the full range of subjects? Do some pupils with emotional and behavioural difficulties need a modified curriculum with more time for activities such as drama, art and craft, or music which could be seen as having a therapeutic value? In some cases, where behaviour is profoundly disturbed, a developmental curriculum which is more concerned with social than academic goals may be more appropriate.

Traditionally, special schools have offered modified or developmental curricula but nowadays the National Curriculum is seen as an entitlement for all. *The Education of Children with Emotional and Behavioural Difficulties* (DFE, 9/94) does, however, acknowledge that some leeway is necessary, as special schools tend to be small and to cater for a wide range of age, ability and social functioning: 'the National Curriculum may have to be planned by the school in conjunction with the other provision to be made for the education, care and personal development of the individual pupil' (DFE, 9/94 paragraph 65). Similarly, *The Education by LEAs of Children Otherwise than at School* (DFE, 11/94) concedes that pupil referral units (PRUs) providing education for pupils excluded from mainstream schools 'are not bound to provide the full National Curriculum because of their varied and different circumstances' (DFE, 11/94 paragraph 38).

Whether in mainstream or special school or unit, there will be some tension between academic and therapeutic objectives for teaching pupils with problems. What can be done to resolve it? *Pupil Behaviour and Discipline* (DFE, 8/94) suggests that the starting point for an effective curriculum can be seen in certain characteristics of classroom management in successful schools. These are summarized below, together with some references to studies which offer more specific advice on how schools and teachers can be encouraged to develop these characteristics.

Procedures, rules and routines are rational and clearly understood

Established procedures for participating in lessons help promote a calm and purposeful classroom atmosphere. Rules define the boundaries for behaviour and routines regulate the flow of activities. Rationality is important because as the Elton Report (DES, 1989) noted, 'obscure, arbitrary and petty rules discredit the whole code'. Clarity of understanding is important because, as McManus (1989) points out, pupils will always test out rules and 'the less specific and convincing the teacher, the more they will explore the boundaries of what they suspect to be permissible'.

Rogers (1991) emphasizes the value of engaging pupils in formulating rules for themselves but also suggests six areas which these will usually cover:

- communication including procedures for taking turns and regulating hurtful or offensive language
- conflict settlement and arrangements for resolving disputes through negotiation
- movement and routines for entering, leaving and moving around the classroom
- safety and the use of equipment
- learning and routines for gaining attention and support, if necessary
- treatment and respect for other people.

Instructions, tasks and goals are clearly explained and work matched to pupil ability

As Lovitt (1977) memorably commented, most children, 'if they know what we want them to do, will do it'. Far more problems arise from confusion about instructions than from wilful refusal to follow them. Kyriacou (1991) provides very helpful checklists of key questions for teachers to ask themselves on lesson preparation and management and argues that, in setting tasks, it is crucial to:

- indicate the relationship between the work involved and the learning intended
- carefully prepare tasks and materials
- give a clear briefing on what is required before starting an activity
- match work to pupils' abilities and interests
- use questions to check progress and understanding.

Lessons are smoothly organized, interruptions minimized and misbehaviour handled quickly and calmly

Difficulties in classroom management often escalate from minor irritation to major confrontation. In order to reduce disruption, it is useful to apply what have been described by Smith and Laslett (1993) as the 'four rules' of classroom management: get them in; get them out; get on with it; and get on with them.

- Effective teachers 'get them in' by starting lessons smoothly and promptly, providing short, simple tasks which recap the previous lesson or give pupils a reminder of the skills needed for the next activity.
- Teachers who 'get them out' efficiently, give thought to an orderly routine for concluding lessons, collecting materials and discussing what has been achieved in ways which restate and reinforce the theme of the lesson.
- Teachers 'get on with it' by selecting suitable content, ensuring that methods and materials are appropriate, providing that alternative and supplementary work is available and organizing the classroom so that layout and seating arrangements are suitable.
- Teachers 'get on with them' by building good personal relationships through learning names and gathering information about personal interests so that they become more aware of each pupil as an individual.

Analysing classroom organization, teaching methods and the nature of the curriculum will help schools provide an environment conducive to pupils achieving their potential and this should reduce sources of friction and disaffection. However, for some pupils with problems more intensive individual help is necessary.

MEDIATION AND INDIVIDUAL COUNSELLING

Mediation refers to providing the additional, personal counselling and guidance which some pupils require, to finding ways of enhancing the self-esteem of pupils with problems and managing systems of pastoral care, which safeguard pupil welfare and ensure equal opportunities for progress. Mediation is concerned with the conditions of learning and possibilities of support for individual pupils with problems. What can be done to enhance positive features of classroom life, promote self-esteem and celebrate personal achievement for pupils whose emotional and behavioural difficulties hinder progress in learning?

Exclusions from School (DFE, 10/94) stresses the necessity of considering incidents of poor behaviour not only in relation to school behaviour policies and the criminal law but also in relation to other factors concerning the circumstances of the particular incident, its effect on others and its impact on the life of the school and 'any particular circumstances unique to the pupil'. Though mainly covering legal requirements and procedures, this circular strongly underlines the official view that exclusion should be kept to a minimum and permanent exclusion used only as a genuine last resort after all reasonable steps have been taken to avoid it. Attention is drawn to considering whether poor behaviour might be an 'emerging sign of an emotional and behavioural difficulty giving rise to a special educational need'.

Effective discussions with pupils

Teachers applying the management strategies outlined above may still encounter some pupils whose behaviour is unacceptable. The first step for dealing with this problem is an extension of the fourth rule of classroom management: 'getting on with them'. Often the problem can be resolved simply by having a quiet talk which seeks to discover why a pupil finds disruption more rewarding than co-operative behaviour. This should not be taken as an opportunity for a private 'telling off', though that technique also has its place at an earlier stage. Here the teacher is using discussion to explore the pupil's reasons or rationalizations for misbehaviour and therefore seeking to open doors to communication rather than to effect an immediate change. It is demonstrating an interest and concern for the pupil as an individual whose perception of events is valued. This approach may not appeal to all teachers and it is important that schools and teachers consider their beliefs about discipline in this context for 'unless teachers find that they have their hearts in whatever form of intervention they adopt, no intervention is likely to succeed' (Smith and Laslett, 1993).

Wolfgang and Glickman (1986) review a range of strategies for managing behaviour and analyse the psychological theories which underpin them. They suggest that there are three schools of thought about discipline:

- The 'Relationship–Listening' school takes the view that the teacher should have faith in the pupil's ability to wrestle with, and solve, problems. The teacher counsels by listening, reflecting back feelings, avoiding judgement or direction.
- The 'ConfrontingContracting' school takes the view that the teacher should make the pupil aware of what are acceptable and unacceptable behaviours. The teacher counsels by confronting the child with the consequences of his or her actions and working out a plan or contract for improvement.
- The 'Rules–Rewards–Punishment' school takes the view the teacher should provide a controlled environment changing rewards or punishments so that the pupil's behaviour is modified.

For the approach to discussion suggested above to work effectively, the teacher will need to be willing to try the 'relationship-listening', non-judgmental approach, asking questions which encourage further comment from the pupil and refraining from directive advice. Some teachers, who might not be happy to work in this way, may prefer to treat discussion with pupils as a directive interaction, adopting the 'confrontation–contracting' approach. Here the discussion becomes an opportunity to face the pupil with what is wrong about current behaviour and to formulate a plan for dealing with it. The essential point is that the purpose of the discussion is clearly identified in the teacher's mind.

Considering strategies in this way suggests that counselling could be seen as a staged approach, trying the non-directive before the directive approach and distinguishing the counselling role from the application of systems of 'rules–rewards–punishment'. This can be helped by developing a role for a member of staff as a school counsellor, consultation with whom offers an alternative to a more traditional disciplinary route for pupils with problems. Cooper (1993) describes how one school has used a school counsellor very effectively but stresses the counsellor's ready admission that without the already positive climate of teacher-pupil relationships in the school, the counselling programme would have been a non-starter.

Positive thinking in the classroom

In promoting such a climate the 'ecosystemic' approach offers helpful advice on how teachers can re-interpret oppositional behaviour by 'reframing' a situation in a more positive way. This approach is based on the concept of the school as a social web rather like a biological ecosystem, in which changes result from a variety of interactions. Cooper, Smith and Upton (1994) explain how the ecosystemic approach developed by Molnar and Lindquist (1989) offers a means of changing problem behaviour, not by challenging the behaviour overtly, but by utilizing the systemic principles which sustain interactional patterns. One of the major aims of this approach is to assist teachers in redefining behaviour, in terms which lead both teacher and perpetrator to see the behaviour as co-operative rather than negative. Deprived of a barrier against which to kick, behaviour loses its original appeal and becomes redundant. An example cited by Fontana (1994) might be reinterpreting to the pupil, or 'reframing' in Molnar and Lindquist's terminology, an action such as calling out in class not as deviant behaviour but, 'as a helpful attempt to contribute further information or to seek clarification of what the teacher is saying'. Whether correct or not, the teacher's newly positive interpretation removes any value the action might have as an act of defiance.

Other techniques for thinking differently about problems derived from Molnar and Lindquist are:

- 'sleuthing' or thinking of a classroom behaviour problem as a mystery to be solved by constructing and trying out new theories until the case is solved
- 'positive connotation of motive' or attributing positive reasons for apparently negative behaviours, e.g. slow work reframed as painstaking
- 'positive connotation of function' or identifying positive aspects of apparently negative behaviour, e.g. silliness reframed as entertainment
- 'symptom prescription' or accepting a problem behaviour but prescribing its performance in a different way, e.g. complaints reframed as suggestions to be written down and discussed after a lesson.

Developing pupil self-esteem

Approaches to mediation described above have mostly been applied in mainstream schools but can be used in special schools and units as well. However, it is likely that children in such schools may need additional help to develop and restore self-esteem.

71

Robinson and Maines (1988) argue that the way people feel about themselves, their self-concept has three aspects:

a) self-image or the internal picture someone has of themselves
b) ideal self or someone's impression of what they would like to be
c) self-esteem which is formed when someone matches these two pictures.

For pupils who have frequently experienced failure, which is likely to be the case for many children in special schools and units, self-esteem will be low, feelings of inadequacy will lead to a lack of confidence in trying new strategies for learning, and behaviour will be consistent with low expectations.

Robinson and Maines offer a series of teaching strategies or 'bag of tricks' which they have found helpful in building up the self-esteem of pupils with problems:

- *label the act*: express displeasure with the behaviour not the child and maintain self-esteem by indicating that such behaviour is surprising in such a normally good pupil
- *take the risk of failure from the child*: let the pupil know that any blame for not getting something right belongs to the teacher for setting work which is too hard or for not explaining tasks clearly enough
- *pat on the back*: use non-verbal expressions and touch, a smile or literally a pat on the back, to convey approval
- *messages*: feelings about behaviour are best conveyed by teachers explaining the effect a behaviour has on them, using a quietly spoken 'I' rather than a loudly shouted 'you' to begin the message
- *make punishment positive*: when sanctions are necessary, make these as mild as possible and focus on reparation not retribution.

A great advantage of approaches based on mediation is that they are not intrusive; because they are applied with individuals, they can be used flexibly and tailored to different teaching and learning styles. The same is not true of systems based on rewards and sanctions designed to modify behaviour which, for consistency and predictability, require an agreed policy for their application throughout a school.

MODIFICATION AND CHANGING BEHAVIOUR

Modification refers to understanding the ways in which learning and standards of behaviour can be modified, changed and improved by discipline policies which offer suitable incentives and appropriate sanctions. Modification is a term most familiar from behavioural psychology and it is concerned with the antecedents and consequences of learning. Here it has a rather broader application than simply applying learning theory to classroom practice. How do schools and individual teachers respond to pupils with problems? What events may precipitate misbehaviour and which approaches to discipline most effectively shape and maintain good behaviour?

As applied in schools, behaviour modification means that problems are described in terms of observable behaviour rather than in statements about a child's personality or attitudes. Observing and recording what happens in the classroom provides the information for planning interventions designed to change behaviour.

Specifying and measuring behaviour

This begins with defining behaviour in a clear and specific way. Bull and Solity (1987) argue that 'the behavioural approach and its concern with the observable can help us to make sure that our own reactions to events and our communication of these to others are as accurate as possible'. Imprecise or 'fuzzy' descriptions of a behaviour make it difficult to record, therefore 'target' behaviour has to be defined in terms of actions that can be seen, and agreed to be seen, by separate observers.

The next step in a programme of behaviour modification is recording the frequency, duration or intensity of the 'target' behaviour. This will provide a 'baseline' against which the success can be measured. Sometimes, recording in itself, particularly if pupils are aware of what is being observed and whether it is viewed favourably or not, may lead to changes in behaviour. Simply counting the number of times a behaviour occurs may reassure a teacher that a problem is not so bad as it appears to be. After a baseline has been established an intervention is then tried and the same behaviours measured to see whether there has been any improvement.

Analysing cues and consequences

A cue is a signal which prompts or guides a course of action. Bull and Solity (1987) analyse three components of the classroom environment which cue particular behaviours:

- The physical component is the classroom and its layout.
- The social component is the teaching style and grouping arrangements.
- The educational component is the curriculum and learning tasks.

The statement of clear rules and expectations combined with the establishment of a series or tariff of consequences for non-compliance associated with 'assertive teaching' (Canter and Canter, 1976) is another aspect of arranging cues to shape appropriate behaviour from pupils and this approach is discussed later in relation to monitoring.

Consequences are the events which reinforce behaviours. Positive reinforcement occurs when events that follow a behaviour strengthen its frequency, duration and intensity. Skilful teachers give effective rewards and arrange pleasant consequences without resort to what Wheldall and Merrett (1992) dub 'behavioural overkill' in the use of heavy, intrusive reinforcers which are difficult to maintain. In schools reinforcement starts with approval and praise and resorts, only if necessary, to tangible reinforcement and aims to fade that out as soon as possible. As Rogers (1991) puts it, 'the ultimate goal of all external reinforcement is the natural reinforcement enjoyed as a result of appropriate behaviours' (p. 197).

Effective reinforcement is contingent upon clearly stated performance targets and will be most powerful if it follows the target behaviour as soon as possible. Although it is easy enough to offer praise, 'thank you for putting up your hand', 'I like the way you're working quietly', 'Well done', it is not so easy to deliver a tangible reinforcement immediately, but using tokens, such as stars or points to be exchanged later for a reward, can be an acceptable alternative. For some children a more formal behavioural contract may be necessary. Usually this involves the teacher arranging a specific reward such as extra time on a favoured activity which is made contingent upon the pupil's improved work performance, greater punctuality or some other reasonable and attainable target. This agreement is then written out and signed by all parties.

Evaluating effective modification

In behavioural psychology, punishment occurs when aversive, unpleasant events follow a behaviour with the intention of reducing its occurrence. Punishment may be necessary to suppress or deter the misbehaviour in the short term. However, though sometimes effective in stopping a bad behaviour, punishment alone will never start a good one and there are other side effects which require consideration.

- If teachers get their own way by being hurtful to others, pupils may 'model' this behaviour.
- Emotionally, punishment is likely to evoke dislike and anxiety causing children to become uncooperative and unwilling to contribute to lessons.
- Children may learn ways to avoid punishment through deceit or cheating or try to escape a threatening situation by not turning up for lessons.

For these reasons punishment does not find favour in behavioural theory except as a last resort to buy time and opportunity for a more positive approach. If the use of punishment is increasing then, whatever the initial intention, it is not being effective. This may be because, however unpleasant it was meant to be, in practice its effect is outweighed, perhaps through 'unofficial reinforcement' from the response of other pupils. To respond to this by increasing the harshness of the punishment will further heighten an antagonistic classroom atmosphere.

In any evaluation of a programme of behaviour modification, the object of the exercise is to make teaching and learning more pleasant and enjoyable. If the teacher is enjoying the experience then the pupil probably will be too, but the opposite is also true. Evaluation should show that investment of time and energy is producing a good return in academic achievement, social competence and improvement in the classroom climate. In other words, the implementation of a behavioural approach should have rewards for the teacher as well as for the pupil. If this is not happening, if the teacher feels that too much time is spent recording and too little time communicating, or that the distribution of tokens is becoming a source of dispute or that too frequently punishments exceed rewards, then the modification programme has to be reviewed and reassessed.

Rogers (1994) writing about mainstream programmes in a primary school setting, offers a plan for 'behaviour recovery':

- Establish a behaviour profile, based on records and observations, to identify targets for improvement
- Explain purpose, model or mirror the inappropriate behaviour, emphasizing its effect on others so the child 'sees' what's wrong
- Model new behaviours, explain the plan and how success will be measured
- Rehearsal by pupil, feedback from teacher supporting the new plan, so the child 'knows' what's right

- Encourage and reward the new behaviour in the classroom, sometimes using other children as 'plan helpers'.

With suitable adaptation, this could equally well be used as a plan for pupils of other ages and for pupils at various stages of assessment under the Code of Practice. At Stage 1, the classroom teacher would be responsible for drawing up the plan but it could equally well be used as a design for intervention involving the SENCO at Stage 2 or a support teacher or psychologist at Stage 3.

The combination of the language and approach of behaviour modification with the mediation through counselling is another interesting feature of Rogers's scheme. This illustrates the point that, in helping pupils with problems, contributions from behavioural and humanistic psychology can be seen not as exclusive and competing theories but as complementary techniques. Ayers, Clarke and Murray (1995) give further examples of how behavioural, ecosystemic and other theoretical perspectives can be applied in the classroom. Effective *monitoring* ensures that teachers have access to a full repertoire of such techniques and a variety of possible responses to pupils with problems.

MONITORING THE EFFECTIVENESS OF SCHOOL POLICIES

Monitoring refers to checking the implementation of school policies on discipline and pastoral care and the role of senior management in helping colleagues cope with problems in classroom management, individual mediation and modifying pupil behaviour. Monitoring is concerned with the effectiveness of school policies. How do schools take account of the needs of pupils with problems when framing and implementing their school development plans or preparing for OFSTED (Office For Standards in Education) inspection? What is done to see that schools do encourage their staff in maintaining positive expectations of these pupils, presenting good models of behaviour and offering feedback on how their conduct is improving?

Pupil Behaviour and Discipline (DFE, 8/94) is mainly about monitoring school performance and the roles which parents, heads, teachers and governors can play in developing and reviewing their behaviour policies. It reflects to a considerable extent the findings of the Elton Report on discipline in schools (DES, 1989) and the OFSTED publication on achieving good behaviour in schools, gleaned from observation of good practice (OFSTED, 1993).

Whole-school policies

Effective schools manage pupil behaviour through a whole-school approach, which promotes respect for all members of the school community, takes firm action to discourage bullying and harassment and works actively to reduce levels of truancy and to prevent poor behaviour in school from leading to exclusion. Although attention is drawn to the importance of schools having regard to the Code of Practice, particularly concerning pupils with emotional and behavioural difficulties, Circular 8/94 is mainly focused on suggesting general principles for maintaining order and fostering good behaviour.

> Good behaviour and discipline are key foundations of good education. Without an orderly atmosphere effective teaching and learning cannot take place. If children are permitted to misbehave at school, or to absent themselves from it, they prejudice their own educational chances. Worse, they disrupt the education of the children around them. (DFE 8/94 p. 6)

It is likely that all pupils, including those with problems, will benefit from working in an environment where teachers subscribe to this view. There is, however, a possibility that this could be taken to imply that children whose behaviour does prejudice the educational chances of themselves or others might best be removed, with a view to improving the orderliness of the atmosphere. Although this is clearly not the intention of this circular or the package as a whole, more specific advice on how to lay these 'key foundations' would have been helpful at this point. For example, schools might be urged to follow the OFSTED (1993) advice and develop whole-school behaviour policies which include:

1 *aims*, which reflect a consensus on values linked to the School Development Plan; which set the moral, spiritual and social ethos of the school; and establish a commitment to equal opportunities for all, including children with special educational needs

2 *quality of teaching and learning*, which reflect high expectations and opportunities for achievement for all pupils, again with an emphasis on inclusion of pupils with special educational needs

3 *an environment* (with systems for support and guidance) which reflects an endeavour to ensure that the school is a pleasant place to be, at lunch and break time as well as during lessons, and where pastoral care is more than a crisis response mechanism for dealing with behaviour problems

4 *rewards* in which all pupils feel they have an opportunity to participate; *sanctions* which are rational and understood

5 *strategies* which deter bullying and harassment, from which pupils with special needs may suffer disproportionately.

Within this framework, monitoring should take particular account of recording, under each heading, the particular interests of pupils with problems, checking for example under aims whether policies on setting and streaming are safeguarding equal opportunities; under quality of teaching and learning whether Individual Educational Plans do have appropriately high expectations for pupils with special needs; whether under environment, sanctions and bullying certain pupils' names feature with undue frequency.

Identifying special educational needs

Sometimes schools have developed separate systems for discipline or pastoral care and support for special educational needs. This can result in pupils moving upwards through a series of disciplinary interventions to the point at which outside specialist help is sought or exclusion considered, without the carefully planned and recorded system of staged assessment required by the Code of Practice. At this point the 'disruptive' pupil has sometimes in the past metamorphosed into a pupil with emotional and behavioural difficulties, in order to qualify for additional assistance, external support or alternative placement. This is not as likely to be forthcoming in a system which demands appropriate documentation.

One of the anxieties voiced by teachers about the new Code of Practice is the danger that its procedures will become unwieldy and overly bureaucratic with an emphasis on legalistic niceties at the expense of flexibility. In the context of the present discussion however, it is surely a matter of good practice to see that behaviour problems are not treated in isolation from learning difficulties. Special Educational Needs Co-ordinators are also most likely to be aware of strategies for early and effective intervention in helping pupils with emotional and behavioural difficulties. *The Education of Children with Emotional and Behavioural Difficulties* (DFE, 9/94) makes it clear that schools should use the school-based stages of assessment to the benefit of the child by taking appropriate action at the first sign of a pattern of difficulty, recording detailed observations and exploring the nature of the difficulty. This view is reinforced by *Exclusions from School* (DFE, 10/94) which argues that 'prompt recognition of children's difficulties, and the commencement where appropriate of the school-based stages may alleviate the child's difficulties and avoid the need for a later exclusion'.

First signs of a pattern of difficulty are likely to be indicated by the frequency with which a child's name crops up for detention or referral to a senior member of staff as a result of regular misdemeanours. It is important at this stage that schools monitor the discipline system before assuming that frequent application of sanctions necessarily implies individual psychopathology. Sometimes the problem may indicate inappropriate application by teachers as much as inappropriate behaviour from pupils.

For example, *Assertive Discipline* (Canter and Canter, 1976) is an approach based on a system of rewards as well as sanctions but its most distinctive element is a hierarchy of consequences for non-compliance with rules governing behaviour in the classroom. For a first transgression a name is recorded on the board with ticks against it added for further misbehaviour within the lesson. Each additional mark adds an additional period of detention or other punishment and for a certain number of minor misbehaviours or immediately for more extreme misbehaviour, the pupil is sent to a senior member of staff, with further consequences such as a letter home to parents.

This system, or variants of it, will certainly identify quickly signs of a pattern of difficulty, but schools should monitor patterns of staff as well as of pupil behaviour. Some teachers may resort more rapidly than others to the sanctions within the system without making use of rewards. Sometimes an individual pupil's 'pattern of difficulty' may only appear in lessons with particular teachers. Given that these possibilities have been discounted, this is the point at which registration at Stage 1 of the Code of Practice becomes appropriate. What this should mean is the avoidance of a gap between the work of school departments or support teams responsible for special needs and school departments or support teams responsible for pastoral care.

SUMMARY

It is essential that describing needs and the resources to meet them should not become a process for labelling or stereotyping children. If that happens teachers and administrators can lose sight of the individual behind the characteristics of the label or condition. Decisions about whether pupils with problems can be helped best in mainstream or special provision will always depend on individual circumstances. By using the conceptual framework offered by the four 'Ms', schools and services can deploy a range of possible practical classroom-based strategies in responding to the administrative guidelines provided by the *Pupils With Problems* package.

REFERENCES

Ayers, H., Clarke, D. and Murray, A. (1995) *Perspectives on Behaviour: A Practical Guide to Effective Interventions for Teachers*. London: David Fulton.

Bull, S.L. and Solity, J.E. (1987) *Classroom Management: Principles to Practice*. London: Croom Helm.

Canter, L. and Canter, M. (1976) *Assertive Discipline: A Take Charge Approach for Today's Education*. Seal Beach, CA: Canter and Associates.

Cooper, P. (1993) *Effective Schools for Disaffected Students: Integration and Segregation*. London: Routledge.

Cooper, P., Smith, C.J. and Upton, G. (1994) *Emotional and Behavioural Difficulties: Theory to Practice*. London: Routledge.

DES (1989) *Discipline in Schools* (The Elton Report). London: HMSO.

DFE (1994) *Pupils with Problems* (Pack of six linked circulars) London: HMSO.

DFE (1994a) *Pupil Behaviour and Discipline*. Circular 8/94. London: HMSO.

DFE (1994b) *The Education of Children with Emotional and Behavioural Difficulties*. Circular 9/94. London: HMSO.

DFE (1994c) *Exclusions from School*. Circular 10/94. London: HMSO.

DFE (1994d) *The Education by LEAs of Children Otherwise than at School*. Circular 11/94. London: HMSO.

DFE (1994e) *The Education of Sick Children*. Circular 12/94. London: HMSO.

DFE (1994f) *The Education of Children being Looked after by Local Authorities*. Circular 13/94. London: HMSO.

Fontana, D. (1994) *Managing Classroom Behaviour*. Leicester: BPS Books.

Kyriacou, C. (1991) *Essential Teaching Skills*. Hemel Hempstead: Simon & Schuster Education.

Lovitt, T.C. (1977) *In Spite of My Resistance, I've Learned from Children*. Columbus, OH: Merrill.

McManus, M. (1989) *Troublesome Behaviour in the Classroom: A Teacher's Survival Guide*. London: Routledge.

Molnar, A. and Lindquist, B. (1989) *Changing Problem Behaviour in Schools*. San Francisco: Jossey-Bass.

OFSTED (1993) *Achieving Good Behaviour in Schools*. London: DFE.

Robinson, G. and Maines, B. (1988) *They Can Because They Think They Can*. Maidstone: AWMC; and *A Bag of Tricks* (Video and Workbook). Portishead: Lame Duck Enterprises.

Rogers, W.A. (1991) *'You Know The Fair Rule': Strategies for Making the Hard Job of Discipline in School Easier*. Harlow: Longman.

Rogers, W.A. (1994) *Behaviour Recovery: A Whole-School Program for Mainstream Schools*. Harlow: Longman.

Smith, C.J. (1991) Behaviour management: a whole school policy. In M. Hinson (ed.) *Teachers and Special Educational Needs: Coping with Change* (2nd edn). London: Longman.

Smith, C.J. and Laslett, R. (1993) *Effective Classroom Management: A Teacher's Guide* (2nd edn). London: Routledge.

Wheldall, K. and Merrett, F. (1992) Effective classroom behaviour management: positive teaching. In K. Wheldall (ed.) *Discipline in Schools: Psychological Perspectives on the Elton Report*. London: Routledge.

Wolfgang, C.H. and Glickman, C.D. *Solving Discipline Problems: Strategies for Classroom Teachers* (2nd edn). Boston: Allyn and Bacon.

CHAPTER 7

The Management of Behaviour Problems in Children with Learning Disabilities

Harinder Mohan Verma

The terms 'learning disabilities', 'mental retardation', 'learning difficulties' and 'mental handicap' are used interchangeably and signify the same underlying condition. 'Learning disability' is a term adopted by the Department of Health in Great Britain and will be used here. It is a condition of arrested or incomplete development of mind which is characterized by reduced level of intellectual functioning resulting in impaired ability to adapt to the daily demands of the social environment. The disability must be recognizable at birth or before the age of 18 years. The IQ level on its own should not be applied rigidly and the global assessment of ability should include the influence of commonly associated physical or mental disorders on the clinical picture and the performance. There are four broad categories of learning disabilities based on IQ level: mild (IQ 50–64), moderate (IQ 35–49), severe (IQ 20–34) and profound (IQ under 20).

Learning disability is often associated with various secondary conditions including psychological problems, epilepsy, sensory deficit/impairment, speech and mobility problems. In the population of persons with learning disabilities, psychological impairment ranks second only to mobility limitation in observed occurrence of secondary disabilities (Jacobson and Janicki, 1987). Such problems include aggression, self-injurious and destructive behaviours, oppositional and defiant behaviour, hyperactivity, screaming, absconding and sleep problems. When such behaviours disrupt an individual's or carer's life severely and start presenting a degree of risk to self or others (thereby affecting the quality of life) they are often described as challenging behaviours. The associated communication deficit and linguistic incompetence in many such individuals hinder the formulation of a reliable psychological profile. This makes it imperative for professionals working with children with learning disabilities to acquaint themselves with the recent advances in psycholinguistic knowledge.

PSYCHOLINGUISTIC FACTORS

Much of the material about the pragmatics of expressive language and inner representation of linguistic concepts has been distilled from the related literature on autism. Leudar (1989) highlighted the difficulties in understanding intentions resulting from incoherence of discourse and the conduct of interaction. The violation of communicative conventions has shown a strong relationship between communicative environment and behaviour disturbances, like antisocial behaviour, and loneliness. Frith (1989a, b) describes the concept of 'second order' representation in understanding autistic aloofness. An infant forms 'first order' representation of routinely encountered objects and categories as cups and hats which contain information about their physical appearance and properties. This may be impaired in some children with learning disability. The second order representation is a critical ingredient in the ability to pretend and in many other accomplishments, including mentalizing – that is, thinking and reasoning about the content of our own and other people's minds. The systematic mentalization is due to a 'theory of mind' which is a spin-off from the development of the concept of second order representation. Such an ability is essential in order to understand the state of mind of other people through observing their actions and through applying one's past experience of causes and effects in similar situations, and for a meaningful two-way communicative-social interaction. A defect in second order representation and thus an inability to read the mind-intention of the listener may result in a disharmony leading to withdrawal of the autistic person or to loss of control. There is, however, a need to be cognizant of the fact that language and communication deficits are also an integral part of learning disabilities.

In people with learning disabilities inappropriate forms of speech are used in gaining access to conversation. This is partly due to their innate linguistic difficulties and immaturity and partly because of deficits in social cognition. As the child grows, normal strategies are learned through negotiation between conversational participants. Difficulties in developing these negotiating skills would result in people with learning disabilities adopting a passive role in conversation. Mitchell (1987) has highlighted the role of parents in ensuring appropriate interactions with children with severe learning disabilities. Of equal relevance is the state of a child's arousal level which determines the degree of learning that takes place, and this may be so variable that no accurate predictions are possible.

BIOLOGICAL AND RELATED FACTORS

However, linguistic skills are influenced by a variety of biological, sociological and psychological variables which determine links between behaviour and communication. Hagberg, Hagberg, Lewerth and Lindberg (1981) noted that in their study a high proportion of children with learning disabilities had associated neurological handicaps. Adverse obstetric factors are likely to result in poor development of communication skills. The concept of minimum brain dysfunction (MBD) invites controversy but it has a validity in being used as a term to describe a constellation of signs and symptoms (Rasmussen *et al.*, 1982). Population-based surveys (Drillien *et al.*, 1980;

Rao, 1990) have confirmed that there is a stronger association between mild learning disabilities and biological causes than was generally believed to exist. It is likely that the resultant distortions in the neuronal maturation synapse formation and imbalance in neurotransmitter in the developing brain could have a direct effect on perceptual–attentional–communicative function (Patel and Lewis, 1982). This may have consequences for the adaptive behaviour of people with learning disabilities.

CUMULATIVE FACTORS

In addition to the difficulties of language, there are a number of factors within the world of a child with learning disabilities which influence the behavioural pattern. There is emerging evidence to suggest a strong relationship between chronic disease and vulnerability to behavioural and emotional problems (Eiser, 1990). Intrapersonal, interpersonal and social-ecological factors have been highlighted by Wallender, Varni, Balani, Banis and Wilcox (1988). Severity of learning disability and multiplicity of associated disabilities affect psychological comorbidity, and therefore attention deficit disorder, autism, conduct disorder, epilepsy, anxiety, phobias and depression are very common. Accordingly the concept of dual diagnosis (learning disabilities and superimposed behaviour/psychiatric problems) has lately gained increasing credence. A family with a child with learning disabilities is more exposed to stressful situations; there may be a reciprocal effect. Such a family is at a greater risk of maladjustment. Gath, 1978; Byrne and Cunningham, 1985; Dupont, 1986; Fredrich, 1979 all address issues like temperament and coping style of the mother and social-ecological factors like marital and family functioning and social-economic network and resources.

Additional physical problems like cardiac disease, hearing impairments or cleft palate are likely to increase the rate of associated behaviour problems by at least two to three times (Heller, Rafman, Zvagulis and Pless, 1985). Brain-damaged children have severe longstanding problems, especially in the area of learning disabilities and social isolation while children with cystic fibrosis showed improved adjustment over a five-year period of study (Breslau and Marshall, 1985). Goodyer, 1990 has reviewed the importance of life events and family relationships to childhood psychopathology. A child with learning disability is likely to suffer more stress in the form of early separations through hospitalizations. Experience of being an infant is prolonged and communications fail through aberrant and unsuccessful crying (Fraser and Ozols, 1980, 1981). The experience of being unable to communicate pain, discomfort and temperature, and feeding and sleeping distortions of biological equilibrium must affect the early life patterns more stressfully for a child with profound learning disabilities. The term 'hassle' is used by Gallimore, Weisner, Koffman and Bernheimer (1989) to describe the effect of sleep problems, poor communication skills, physical limitations and extreme behaviour problems on a family's functioning. Families with 'low hassle' children were not much dissimilar to those with normal children. Families with 'high hassle' developmentally-delayed children will show heavier mother workload, greater engagement of siblings in child care and increased likelihood of mother's deferring employment or career development.

Clements, Wing and Dunn (1986) show that sleep problems are more common in children with learning disabilities and in a vicious circle this has a very strong association with maternal stress. Poor communication skills result in frustration for child and parent and thus cause irritability (Quine, 1986; Leudar, Fraser and Jeeves, 1987).

A young person with learning disabilities is likely to reach adolescence without the acquisition of social cognition due to relative lack of optimal communicative environment at school. Such a child with a social world described as 'a baffling and problem-strewn battleground' by Beveridge and Conti-Ramsden (1987) is likely to respond either by becoming hostile and aggressive or by being non-assertive and deferential.

FAMILY ADJUSTMENT FACTORS

The association between the aforementioned factors and resultant behaviour problems is complex and warrants further carefully conducted research in order to establish cause–effect relationships. There is, however, a wealth of research literature on stress in the families of children with learning disabilities. The importance of the daily caretaking burden (Gowen, Johnston-Martin, Goldman and Applebaum, 1989), however, shows that maternal well-being is not adversely affected simply by having a child with learning disabilities. Parents' values based on social resources, experience and perception of disability are important determining factors. Flynt and Wood (1989) reported that both Black mothers and older mothers have a lower perception of stress than white mothers and younger mothers, possibly due to more social support. Parental belief systems are known to massively influence the perception of stress, family adjustment and psychological well-being as shown by Frey *et al.* (1989). 'Getting through the day – the sustainability of everyday activities – seems to predict better child and family adjustment than does the level of stimulation of the child (Gallimore *et al.*, 1989). They use the term ecocultural niche – 'econiche' (Super and Harkness, 1986) – to refer to the family's collective action to accommodate to a child with learning disabilities; it is influenced by parental beliefs and goals and manifests in daily routines necessary to modify the stresses placed upon the family. A competitive frame of reference – 'at least she is not as handicapped as . . . ' – is an important way of coping. A problem-focus coping style was related to less psychological distress, wishful thinking to higher stress. Perceived 'control' is important for maternal psychological well-being. Children with Down syndrome have been found to have dampened affect and thus provide fewer cues to care-givers (Bridges and Cicchetti, 1982; Gunn and Berry, 1985). Mothers will fulfil this role of what Mills, Puckering, Pound and Cox's 1985 study called 'a link of reciprocal activity between mother and child' (an episode of activity containing both content – introduction or expression of material to discuss – and context of what must be relevant to the child's ongoing behaviour). Depressed mothers make fewer links. Mothers of children with learning disabilities are not universally more depressed but where they are the effect will be considerable both on mother–infant relations and future child development and behaviour. A child with learning disability will often be less responsive and show less intersubjectivity (Trevarthen, 1980) and the mother will be unable to raise expectations or provide rich and appropriate motherese (Bruner, 1975). In toddlerhood further disappointments may ensue, for example the Down syndrome child may make relatively good progress in the first year followed by poorer acquisition and retention of knowledge later on (Wishart, 1990).

STRATEGIES FOR HELP

Although Howlin and Rutter (1989) caution against claiming too much for the effectiveness of language therapy, yet there is emerging evidence that augmented communication systems do improve attention and intentional communication specifically as highlighted by Abrahamsen, Romski and Sevcik (1989) with their transcript-based analysis of responsivity (STAR). Burford (1988) described engagement techniques involving rhythmic groups of cycle movements ('action cycles') for the profoundly handicapped person displaying a confusing overlay of involuntary movements and producing mannerisms and messages which are possibly intentional. The 'action cycles' were identified by her during interaction between care-giving adults, children and young adults with learning disabilities. These were allocated to five categories according to rate, each action cycle clearly having its own communicative purposes. There is a striking regularity of rate within each performed set of action cycles giving strong indications of a biologically robust system of basic emotional communication which can be tapped into by the care-givers. Thus the improved emotional communication may help in preventing the emergence or perpetuation of maladaptive behaviours. The social context and consequences of communication are equally important variables for consideration. The basic function of communication is to enable an individual to maintain a harmony both internally and with the social world in which the individual exists. The communication, even if it is maladaptive, alters the environment. Many problem behaviours displayed by children with severe and profound learning disabilities may perform a social communicative function. Direct observation and a structured approach of antecedents, resultant behaviour and consequences is essential in order for the interventions to be effective in what can be a complex interaction with the environment. Repp and Felce (1990) have developed a system which allows the recording of up to 45 events on a portable computer (Epson HX 20). These include environmental setting conditions, antecedent events (for example staff demands), consequences (for example staff attention) or target behaviours. This allows environment–behaviour sequences to be analysed and not simply summary estimates, as previously, of the frequency and duration of behaviour disturbances. The concept of conditional probability also must be taken into account. For instance, an environment may be judged therapeutic when it simply does not provide the opportunity for a disturbed behaviour to occur.

PSYCHOLOGICAL THERAPIES

Much of the literature regarding psychological therapies relates to adults with learning disabilities (Allen, 1989; Lindsay and Baty, 1989). However, many of these techniques and the basic concepts behind them are applicable to children and adolescents. In the post-institutional era people with learning disabilities are becoming increasingly exposed to the greater range of opportunities and the inevitable stresses in the ordinary patterns of living in community settings. Consequently, anxiety states, phobias and panic attacks are becoming commoner and a panic situation can create an endangering situation for the individual and others.

Abbreviated progressive relaxation techniques developed by Bernstein and Borkovec (1973) have been used in individuals suffering from chronic anxiety with a significant reduction in both symptoms and disruptive behaviour. There was also concomitant improvement in agitated movement, agitated speech and general anxiety symptoms. Behaviour relaxation training (BRT) is simpler and does not require the subject to tense his or her muscles or perceive and understand the differences between tense and relaxed muscles. Lindsay and Baty (1986a, b) reported this effective both individually and in group situations with people with severe learning disabilities. Similarly, cue-controlled relaxation (CCR) involves relaxation linked to a cue word and can be used to control an initial panic-causing setting such as an asthma attack or a general excited situation. Calamari, Geist and Shahbazian (1987) have used combined relaxation techniques including electromyography, biofeedback, abbreviated progressive relaxation, modelling and positive reinforcement procedures with excellent results. *In vivo* exposure methods have been used in studies of travelling, crossing roads, dogs, with several treatment components like increased contact with the feared situation, changing stimuli, eliciting anxiety, graded exposures, therapist models, non-anxious responses, control over the fearful situation (for example giving the dog orders), generalization and relaxation exercises when necessary. Lindsay recommends the use first of graded exposure for the treatment of phobic anxiety in people with learning disabilities.

An entire range of therapies must be considered in enabling a person with learning disability to be more successful in his or her social environment, and also in helping to decrease an individual's self-injurious behaviours and aggression. Novaco's (1975) approach has been most influential in anger control in persons of normal intellect. It emphasizes cognition, expectations and appraisal of situations. The client is taught the nature and functions of anger, personal triggers and the escalation and vicious circle that ensues; how to review his or her cognition and feelings; and exercises in alternative thoughts and social skills of proper assertiveness. Although this approach might be too complex for people with learning disabilities, Black *et al.* (1988) have been relatively successful in using a modified Novaco technique with people with mild or borderline learning disabilities.

The expansion of interest in cognitive therapies has now reached the people with learning disabilities. Self-instructional training (SIT) based on Meichenbaum's (1977) hypothesis that voluntary behaviour in children is initiated and inhibited by verbal control has now been extended to children and adults with learning disabilities. Lindsay (1986) has reported a series of cases in which the result of social skills training appeared to be related to changes in cognition, the effects of poor self-image and especially a lack of self-confidence. Meichenbaum (1974, 1977) has shown that negative self-statements play an important part in poor coping in social situations. Lindsay and Kasprowicz (1987) have shown that people with learning disabilities can increase their confidence after positive self-statement training. While most studies have focused on people with mild learning disabilities, Rickard *et al.* (1984) have studied people with severe learning disabilities as well.

In some cases the functional analysis of aggressive and self-injurious behaviour in people with learning disabilities does not always reveal plausible or intentional behaviours. The 'out-of-the-blue' episodes of aggression and destructive behaviours sometimes cannot be explained simply by environmentally dependent factors. Such behaviours were in the past described as 'sub-clinical seizures' and 'episodic dyscontrol' (Rickler, 1982; Nunn, 1986). The current term is 'frontal lobe seizure', suggesting that the episodic rage may be involuntary. The person may show specific eye, face, trunk and limb movements with vocalizations accompanied by extreme aggression and destructive behaviours. A simple behaviour modification programme therefore may not prove very effective; however help with appropriate medication may completely change the picture to everybody's advantage.

DRUG TREATMENT

There is evidence that psychotropic medication (tranquillizers) can be used to reduce aggression, self-injurious behaviours and repetitive stereotypic behaviour (Singh and Millichamp, 1985; Craft and Berry, 1987). Aggressive behaviour is one of the most important reasons for commencing someone on a tranquillizer. However, such medication is invariably used without a proper functional analysis of the behaviour in its own environment and without due consideration for the dampening effect on an individual's already limited intellectual abilities. In the last few years a number of new preparations have become available which have much less sedative effect and also have good profile for side effects. Sometimes the aggression and disturbed behaviour can be due to underlying depression or other psychiatric condition which will respond well to appropriate medication. In some cases of severe aggression or self-injurious behaviour, especially when exhibited in a cyclical pattern, drugs like lithium carbonate have been found to be effective (Tyrer *et al.*, 1984). In attention deficit disorders the use of cerebral stimulants is well established, but their use in people with learning disabilities has not been explored. Anticonvulsants like Carbamazepine are thought to be helpful (Langee, 1989) in reducing aggression and self-mutilation, especially when people with learning disabilities have associated seizure disorder. Drugs, however, should only be used as a last resort, always as an adjunct to multidisciplinary assessment and behavioural/psychological intervention, and only under the supervision of a specialist.

ALTERNATIVE THERAPIES

Some alternative therapies are being used increasingly, especially with people with severe learning disabilities. Gentle teaching is a concept which is based on philosophical content using techniques that involve interpreting self-injurious behaviour and redirecting the individual to certain specific meaningful tasks like setting the table. Approximations to the tasks are socially reinforced. McGee *et al.* (1987) feel that 'gentle therapy leads care-givers to teach bonding to those who attempt to distance themselves from meaningful interactions and is aimed at helping individuals with learning disabilities to learn the value and reward of human interaction'. This approach is preferred by most when compared to some of the aversive therapies used in the past. Similarly, aromatherapy is being used increasingly for its relaxing, invigorating and health-promoting effects, to provide sensory stimulation and to help an individual develop communication through a trusting relationship. Stress-related behaviours can be helped through the use of massage with relaxing essential oils. Aromatherapy can offer much to create the kind of supportive and stimulating environment in which the physical, psychological and emotional needs of an individual are met positively. Such therapies espouse the principle of 'ordinary lives for ordinary people' and can improve an individual's quality of life. However, further research and investigation into these therapies is necessary in order to confirm their sustained and proven effectiveness in problem behaviours.

SUMMARY

There is an ever-expanding reservoir of knowledge and research into the problems of people with learning disabilities. It is impossible for any one discipline to gauge the matrix of items which might cause challenging behaviours. First we have to take into account both environmentally dependent factors such as failed communications and aberrant behaviours which have been inadvertently reinforced, and environmentally independent factors such as homeostasis and developmental, organic or functional mental illness (Baumeister, 1989). While trying to help an individual with learning disabilities and superimposed behaviour problems, one needs to take a careful look at the quality of the communicative environment and the social context in which communication failure occurs. A proper behavioural and communicative functional analysis must be carried out. Equally important are the coping abilities of the families, the level of optimal interaction system within the family environment, the perception of the burden of caretaking and the belief systems within the family – all may modulate the quality of interactions. In as far as the specific therapies and interventions are concerned, one needs to borrow heavily from cognitive and other behavioural techniques developed for adults with learning disabilities while taking into account certain newer intervention techniques such as 'engagement'. Most of the literature concerning interventions has been hampered by the relative deficiencies in quantitative measurements of outcomes and the evaluation of the facts. Therefore continued research in these areas is vital to improve the quality of life of people with learning disabilities and help the carers and the families.

REFERENCES

Abrahamsen, A., Romski, M. and Sevcik, R.A. (1989) Concomitants of success in acquiring an augmentative communication system: changes in attention, communication and sociability. *American Journal of Mental Retardation*, **93**, 475–96.

Allen, E.A. (1989) Behavioural treatment of anxiety and related disorders in adults with mental handicap: a review. *Mental Handicap Research*, **2**, 47–60.

Baumeister, A.A. (1989) Causes of severe maladaptive behaviour in persons with severe mental retardation: a review of hypotheses. Paper presented at the National Institutes of Health, Bethesda.

Bernstein, D.A. and Borkovec, T.D. (1973) *Progressive Relaxation Training*. Chicago: Research Press.

Beveridge, M. and Conti-Ramsden, G. (1987) Social cognition and problem-solving in persons with mental retardation. *Australian and New Zealand Journal of Developmental Disabilities*, **13**, 99–106.

Black, I., Cullen, C., Dickens, P. and Turnbull, J. (1988) Anger control. *British Journal of Hospital Medicine*, **40**, 325–9.

Breslau, N. and Marshall, I.A. (1985) Psychological disturbance in children with physical disabilities: continuity and change in a 5-year follow-up. *Journal of Abnormal Child Psychology*, **13**, 199–216.

Bridges, F.A. and Cicchetti, D. (1982) Mothers' ratings of the temperament characteristics of Down syndrome infants. *Developmental Psychology*, **18**, 238–44.

Bruner, J.S. (1975) The ontogenesis of speech acts. *Journal of Child Language*, **2**, 1–19.

Burford, B. (1988) Action cycles: rhythmic actions for engagement with profoundly mentally handicapped children and young adults. *European Journal of Special Needs Education*, **3**, 189– 206.

Byrne, E.A. and Cunningham, C. (1985) The effects of mentally handicapped children on families: a conceptual review. *Journal of Child Psychology and Psychiatry*, **26**, 847–964.

Calamari, J.E., Geist, G.O. and Shahbazian, M.J. (1987) Evaluation of multiple component relaxation training with developmentally disabled persons. *Research in Developmental Abilities*, **8**, 55–70.

Clements, J., Wing, L. and Dunn G. (1986) Sleep problems in handicapped children: a preliminary study. *Journal of Child Psychology and Psychiatry*, **27**, 399–407.

Craft, M. and Berry, I. (1987) The role of the professional in aggression and strategies of coping. In M. Craft, J. Bicknell and S. Hollins (eds) *Mental Handicap: A Multidisciplinary Approach*. London: Bailliere Tindall, pp. 397–409.

Drillien, C.M., Thomson, A.J. and Burgoyne, K. (1980) Low birth weight children in early school age: a longitudinal study. *Developmental Medicine and Child Neurology*, **22**, 26–47.

Dupont, A. (1986) Socio-psychiatric aspects of the young severely mentally handicapped children on families. Blake Marsh Lecture, February 1985. *British Journal of Psychiatry*, **148**, 227–234.

Eiser, C. (1990) Psychological effects of chronic disease. *Journal of Child Psychology and Psychiatry*, **31**, 85–98.

Flynt, S. and Wood, T. (1989) Stress and coping of mothers of children with moderate mental retardation. *American Journal of Mental Retardation*, **94**, 278–83.

Fraser, W. and Ozols, D. (1980) Cries of pain and distress in the severely mentally handicapped. In P. Mittler (ed.) *Proceedings of the 5th Congress of the International Association for the Scientific Study of Mental Deficiency, Jerusalem*, vol. 2. Baltimore: University Park Press, pp. 130–7.

Fraser, W. and Ozols, D. (1981) 'He sounds and looks sore': professionals' evaluations of the profoundly handicapped person's pain and distress signals. In W. Fraser and R. Grieve (eds) *Communicating with Normal and Retarded Children*. Bristol: John Wright, pp. 24–32.

Fredrich, W.N. (1979) Predictors of the coping behavior of mothers of handicapped children. *Journal of Consulting and Clinical Psychology*, **47**, 1140–1.

Frey, K., Greenberg, M. and Fewell, R. (1989) Stress and coping among parents of handicapped children: a multidimensional approach. *American Journal of Mental Retardation*, **94**, 240–9.

Frith, U. (1989a) A new look at language and communication in autism. *British Journal of Disorders of Communication*, **24**, 123–50.

Frith, U. (1989b) *Autism: Explaining the Enigma*. Oxford: Blackwell.

Gallimore, R., Weisner, T., Kaufman, S. and Bernheimer, L. (1989) The social construction of the eco-cultural niches: family accommodation of developmentally delayed children. *American Journal of Mental Retardation*, **94**, 216–30.

Gath, A. (1978) *Down's Syndrome and the Family*. London: Academic Press.

Goodyer, I.M. (1990) Family relationships, life events and childhood psychopathology. *Journal of Child Psychology and Psychiatry*, **31**, 161–92.

Gowen, J., Johnstone-Martin, N., Goldman, B. and Appelbaum, M. (1989) Feelings of depression and parenting competence of mothers of handicapped and nonhandicapped infants: a longitudinal study. *American Journal of Mental Retardation*, **94**, 259–71.

Gunn, P. and Berry, P. (1985) Down's syndrome temperament and maternal response to descriptions of child behavior. *Development Psychology*, **12**, 143–6.

Hagberg, B., Hagberg, G., Lewerth, A. and Lindberg, U. (1981) Mild mental retardation in Swedish school children: prevalence. *Acta Paediatrica Scandinavica*, **70**, 441–4.

Heller, A., Rafman, S., Zvagulis, I. and Pless, I. (1985) Birth defects and psychological adjustment. *American Journal of Diseases of Children*, **139**, 257–63.

Howlin, P. and Rutter, M. (1989) Mothers' speech to autistic children: a preliminary causal analysis. *Journal of Child Psychology and Psychiatry*, **30**, 819–43.

Jacobson, J. and Janicki, M.P. (1987) Needs for professional and generic services within a developmental disability care system. In J.A. Molik and R. Antonck (eds) *Transition on Mental Retardation*, vol. 2. Norwood: Ablex, pp. 23–46.

Langee, H.R. (1989) A retrospective study of mentally retarded patients with behavioural disorders who were treated with carbamazepine. *American Journal of Mental Retardation*, **93**, 640–3.

Leudar, I. (1989) Communicative environments for mentally handicapped people. In M. Beveridge, G. Conti-Ramsden and I. Leudar (eds) *Language and Communication in Mentally Handicapped People*. London: Chapman & Hall, pp. 274–300.

Leudar, I., Fraser, W. and Jeeves, M.A. (1987) Theoretical problems and practical solutions to behaviour disorders in retarded people. *Health Bulletin*, **45**, 347–55.

Lindsay, W.R. (1986) Cognitive changes after social skills training with young mildly mentally handicapped adults. *Journal of Mental Deficiency Research*, **30**, 81–8.

Lindsay, W.R. and Baty, F.J. (1986a) Abbreviated progressive relaxation: its use with adults who are mentally handicapped. *Mental Handicap*, **14**, 123–6.

Lindsay, W.R. and Baty, F.J. (1986b) Behavioural relaxation training: explorations with adults who are mentally handicapped. *Mental Handicap*, **14**, 160–2.

Lindsay, W.R. and Baty, F.J. (1989) Group relaxation training with adults who are mentally handicapped. *Behavioural Psychotherapy*, **17**, 43–51.

Lindsay, W.R. and Kasprowicz, M. (1987) Challenging negative cognitions: developing confidence in adults by means of cognitive behaviour therapy. *Mental Handicap*, **15**, 159–62.

McGee, J.J., Menolascino, F., Hobbs, D. and Menonsch, P.E. (1987) *Gentle Teaching: A Non-aversive Approach to Helping Persons with Mental Retardation*. New York: Human Sciences.

Meichenbaum, D. (1974) Therapist manual for cognitive behaviour modification. Unpublished manuscript. University of Waterloo, Waterloo, Ontario, Canada.

Meichenbaum, D. (1977) *Cognitive Behaviour Modification: An Integrative Approach*. New York: Plenum.

Mills, M., Puckering, C., Pound, A. and Cox, A. (1985) What is it about depressed mothers that influences their children's functioning? In J. Stevenson (ed.) *Recent Advances in Developmental Psychopathology*. Oxford: Pergamon.

Mitchell, D.R. (1987) Parents' interactions with their developmentally disabled or at risk infants: a focus of intervention. *Australian and New Zealand Journal of Developmental Disabilities*, **13**, 73–81.

Novaco, R.W. (1975) *Anger Control: The Development and Evaluation of an Experimental Treatment*. Lexington, MA: Heath.

Nunn, K. (1986) The episodic dyscontrol symptom in childhood. *Journal of Child Psychology and Psychiatry*. **22**, 439–46.

Patel, A.J. and Lewis, P.D. (1982) Effects of proliferation of pharmacological agents acting on the central nervous system. In K.N. Prasad and A. Vernadakis (eds) *Mechanism of Actions of Neurotoxic Substances*. New York: Raven Press, pp. 181–218.

Quine, L. (1986) Behaviour problems in severely mentally handicapped children. *Psychological Medicine*, **16**, 895–907.

Rao, J.M. (1990) A population-based study of mild mental handicap in children: preliminary analysis of obstetric associations. *Journal of Mental Deficiency Research*, **34**, 59–65.

Rasmussen, P., Gillberg, C., Waldenstrom, E. and Svenson, B. (1982) Perceptual, motor and attentional deficits in seven-year-old children: neurological and neurodevelopmental aspects. In *Neuropediatric Aspects of Seven-year-old Children with Perceptual, Motor and Attentional Deficits*. Göteborg: Department of Pediatrics and Clinical Neurophysiology, University of Göteborg, Sweden, pp. 99–128.

Repp, A.C. and Felce, D. (1990) A micro-computer system used for evaluative and experimental behavioural research in mental handicap. *Mental Handicap Research*, **3**, 21–32.

Rickard, H.C., Thrasher, K.A. and Elkins, P.D. (1984) Responses of persons who are mentally retarded to four improvements of retardation instruction. *Mental Retardation*, **22**, 248–52.

Rickler, K.C. (1982) Episodic dyscontrol. In D.F. Benson, D. Blumer and M. Greenblatt (eds) *Psychiatric Aspects of Neurological Disease*, vol. 2. New York: Grune & Stratton, pp. 49–73.

Singh, N.N. and Millichamp, C.J. (1985) Pharmacological treatment of self-injurious behaviour in mentally retarded persons. *Journal of Autism and Developmental Disorders*, **15**, 257–67.

Super, C. and Harkness, S. (1986) The developmental niche: a conceptualisation at the interface of child and culture. *International Journal of Behavioural Development*, **9**, 1–25.

Trevarthen, C. (1980) The foundation of intersubjectivity: development of interpersonal and co-operative understanding in infants. In D. Olson (ed.) *The Social Foundations of Language and Thought; Essays in Honour of J.S. Bruner*. New York: Norton, pp. 316–42.

Tyrer, S.P., Walsh, A., Edwards, D.E., Berney, T.P. and Stephens, D.A. (1984) Factors associated with a good response to lithium in aggressive mentally handicapped subjects. *Progress in Neuro-Psychopharmacology*, **8**, 751–5.

Wallender, J., Varni, J., Balani, L., Banis, H.T. and Wilcox, K.T. (1988) Children with chronic physical disorders: maternal reports of their psychological adjustment. *Journal of Pediatric Psychology*, **13**, 197–212.

Wishart, J.G. (1990) Learning to learn: the difficulties faced by infants and young children with Down's syndrome. In W. Fraser (ed.) *Key Issues in Mental Retardation*. London: Routledge, pp. 249–61.

CHAPTER 8

The Management of Emotional Problems of Children from Ethnic Minorities

Ali EL-Hadi

INTRODUCTION

The aim of this chapter is to highlight some of the theoretical and practical issues which arise in working with children and their families from non-Western ethnic minorities. I shall first review briefly the literature and summarize some of the theoretical issues. Secondly I shall offer some practical guidance and advice to professionals in the field of children's mental health in order to help them avoid misunderstanding and misdiagnosis.

I hope to make clinicians more aware of the specific issues in assessment and management of these children and their families. The focus of this chapter is on children from Asian and African ethnic minorities born to first- or second-generation immigrants from the Indian subcontinent, parts of Africa and the Middle East. I do not include Afro-Caribbean children. My interest stems from my own background. I grew up and received my education up to university level in the Middle East, but all my psychiatric and psychotherapeutic training has been in Britain. In the NHS I work mainly with children of mainstream British origins, but nearly a quarter of the children and the families referred are from the ethnic minorities referred to above. So I shall be drawing on my NHS experience, my private practice in Britain and my Middle East background. The parents of such children are often struggling with feelings of bewilderment and unease when seeking help from the mental health services. The Western-trained professional and the parents are both aware of the cultural gulf which divides them.

Being sensitive to cultural issues and culturally acceptable interventions is more important than the 'right cultural fit' between professional and clients. I believe it is about thinking about difference and diversity. As professionals we often forget that our normative model of the family is a Western one as are the therapeutic interventions which stem from it.

HISTORICAL BACKGROUND

The Office of Population Censuses and Surveys estimated that in 1990 there were over two and a half million people in the UK whose origins were the New Commonwealth. If we were to include migrants from the Irish Republic and mainland Europe, 10 per cent of the population is from an ethnic minority. Contrary to popular perception, half of the non-white population were born in Britain. The history of Asian migration to Britain is well documented, much less so for other non-European ethnic groups. Ballard and Ballard (1977) divided the process of Asian migration into four phases: the first begins in the nineteenth century and the last is the formation of British-born and -educated second-generation Asians. In the 1960s and 1970s the men who had been working in Britain began to bring their wives and children from India, Pakistan and Bangladesh. In the 1970s East African Asians arrived, some voluntarily but others, as in the case of Ugandans, as refugees. Migration from other parts of Africa and the Middle East is less well documented. From 1985 onwards the migrants have been mostly refugees who are fleeing wars or persecution, chiefly from Zaire, Somalia, Sudan, Lebanon, Iraq and Iran. This is a heterogeneous and diverse group with a wide range of cultures, languages and religions. For professionals it is important to bear in mind that the behaviour and attitude of migrant families depend on the events leading to migration, on the migration process itself and on their experience with the host community. Most of those from ethnic minorities live in inner-city areas. In London the figures range from 45 per cent for school-age children in Tower Hamlets to 35 per cent in Redbridge. In Leicester it is 33 per cent.

CULTURE, ETHNICITY AND MENTAL HEALTH

Terms such as 'culture' and 'ethnicity' are not easy to define; it is also difficult to be clear about what is meant by 'mental health'. *Culture* can be seen as all features of an individual's environment, all that a person holds in common with the other individuals who form the same social group. This includes child-rearing practices, family systems, and ethical values and attitudes. *Ethnicity* refers to individuals who belong to the same cultural and racial groups. Members of an ethnic group are thought by themselves and/or others to share a common origin and to share important aspects of culture. *Race* is characterized by physical appearance, is determined by genetic ancestry and is perceived as permanent. Culture and ethnicity are perceived as changeable. Fernando (1991) pointed out that, the term 'mental health' could include the use of medicines for a specific illness or the alleviation of emotional distress in individuals. It could also be about the person's 'inner world', or relationships in the family or society.

Attitudes and beliefs about children's behaviour are aspects of culture and there is a great diversity across cultures. As Hodes (1992) pointed out, different societies have different role expectations; these vary according to age and stage of life and the extent to which either different stages of life are formalized into discrete stages or there is instead a gradual change. Childcare practices vary greatly among families and among people from different societies. This includes things such as the definition of maltreatment, the expression of affection, and play.

The experience of becoming unwell and getting help varies across cultures. People experience distress and symptoms in culture-specific ways (Hodes, 1992). In some cultures people do not distinguish between psychological and physical distress (Kleinman and Good, 1985).

REVIEW OF THE LITERATURE

Children from the ethnic minorities with which we are concerned here are under-represented (with respect to the local population) in referrals to child mental health services. In Tower Hamlets, East London, Stern *et al.* (1990) found only 12 per cent of referrals were from the main ethnic minority (Bangladeshi) when the figure for children from such groups in the local population was 33 per cent. My own research (1993) found a similar picture in Redbridge, East London: 15 per cent of the referrals were of non-Western origin, when the figure from the Commission for Racial Equality (1991 census) was that 39 per cent of the local child population were of non-Western origin. Vyas (1991) found a similar picture in Leicester for Asian children.

Such poor up-take of services is not unique to Britain; it is also documented in the United States (Gibbs *et al.*, 1989). Various explanations have been put forward. Stern *et al.*, (1990) suggested it might be related to the parents' perception of the causes of unwanted behaviours in the children. They referred to Bangladeshi parents' beliefs that such behaviours are caused by 'badness', physical illness and/or 'spirits'. They thought it might also be that the parents do not expect that psychiatric help or service would be available or useful for such problems. Vyas (1991) proposed that one explanation might be remarkable health among Asian children. Indeed, early studies (Kallarckal and Herbert, 1976) found that English children were nearly three times more maladjusted than Indian children. However, more recently Newth (1986) has argued that earlier lower rates of disorder among Asian and immigrant children may have changed. This situation is almost reversed for adults, especially women. Young Asian women are over-represented in suicide and parasuicide statistics for England and Wales.

The question is whether the discrepancy between the under-representation of children in the referrals figures and the over-representation of women in the para-suicide statistics reflect the lack of culturally sensitive or relevant children's mental health services. Stern *et al.* (1990) concluded that the under-representation in the referral figures could not be due to services not meeting the needs of the local population. They cite, to support such a conclusion, the fact that those referrals which reached the service had a broadly similar outcome to referrals of local or indigenous children.

The epidemiological approach to psychiatric disorders which uses a Western system of classification has been criticized by Littlewood (1992) and by Kleinman and Good (1985). Both advocate an anthropological approach which relies on categories and concepts that come from the sufferers and others in their family or network. Such criticisms have been applied to dealings with adult disorders but can also be extended to child disorders. One example here is *anorexia nervosa*. Littlewood and Lipsedge (1987) have argued that it should be regarded as a culture-bound syndrome, in that it requires for its development and manifestation a culture in which thinness is desired.

As Hodes (1992) concluded, there are a number of explanatory models for childhood psychiatric disorders and distress; scientific medicine is only one among many.

DIFFERENT VIEWS AND EXPERIENCES OF CHILDHOOD

Different societies and cultures have their own definitions of childhood, and of the differences between children and adults. There is a great variation across cultures in the extent to which different stages in the life cycle are formalized into discrete stages or whether there is gradual change. For example, adolescence as a more or less distinct stage is a feature of Western industrialized societies. In non-Western and less industrialized societies young people can marry and achieve some form of economic independence at an earlier age, without undergoing a long transitional phase between childhood and adulthood. This is relevant in clinical work with adolescents from ethnic minorities. For the Western-trained professional, it is important during the encounter with family to bear in mind such different and at times opposing views of childhood and of growing-up. This will also include different explanatory models. Child-rearing practices and attitudes associated with childcare and parenting vary greatly across cultures and in different societies. In non-Western cultures child-rearing practices are more relaxed and informal regarding things such as toilet-training, feeding and nurturing, but tend to be more authoritarian regarding discipline and respect for parents and elders. There is less emphasis on separation and auton-omy, in comparison to Western practices. For example, children of primary school age are expected or allowed to sleep with their mothers or in the parental bed. Bedtimes are less formalized and less strict. The extended family setting still common in non-Western cultures allows for multiple mothering, which gives the women in the family a break from childcare without the worries in the Western nuclear family about childminding. Older children are encouraged and expected to participate in household duties and help with the care of younger siblings.

It is important for clinicians who are often asked to assess parenting or family relationships to bear this in mind, and to question their own normative model of family functioning and of parenting.

Case example 1: a 3-year-old Hindu girl

Gurpreet was three when she was referred by her parents. The family are Hindu, originally from India. The young parents were concerned about Gurpreet's non-compliant and defiant behaviour. She frequently had tantrums when they said 'No' to her.

The parents' concerns were shared by the staff of the nursery she attended. The parents admitted that they were at a loss to know how to manage her behaviour, which they described as aggressive and destructive. The parents, who were in their twenties, lived until recently with the extended family, the father's mother and brothers and their respective families. In that household the grandmother was the real authority on child care. When we met with her at a later session she told us that she did not believe adults should say 'No' to a child as young as Gurpreet. Gurpreet's mother who had recently arrived in Britain to marry, did not feel confident enough to challenge her mother-in-law's views or practices. It became clear during the interviews that she did not agree with the grandmother but could not really openly disagree with her.

We worked with them to help them to develop their ideas about setting age-appropriate boundaries for Gurpreet. We also noted that Gurpreet's speech was quite immature for her age, so we arranged for her to have speech therapy. Gurpreet responded well to her parents' consistent management and, as her speech improved with the specific help, there was an overall improvement in her behaviour and concentration. I think that acknowledging the transgenerational boundary issue, without openly challenging it was critical and helped the parents to find their own solution.

Child protection is an area which presents professionals with particular difficulties. This is often the case (and in my own experience) when professionals are making a judgement about whether a particular childcare practice in a family from a different culture is abusive or harmful to children.

During interviews with Asian Bangladeshi families, colleagues and I have observed mothers slapping their infants on their backs while they rocked them to sleep. We were quite taken aback while watching this, and had to be careful not to see it as punitive or a form of physical chastisement, especially as we could see how effective this was in soothing the child into sleep. The variations in childcare practices also apply to the expression of affection and play. In non-Western cultures, and only recently in Western cultures, physical chastisement of children is a common form of discipline. However, it is my own experience that parents from non-Western minorities are particularly vulnerable to being undermined and disempowered by hasty intervention by statutory child-protection interventions.

Case example 2: a Pakistani stepfather

The Khan family was referred by the child-protection team for psychological assessment and possibly therapeutic help. The referral followed a child-protection investigation; the teacher at the school of the two sons, aged nine and seven, reported that they had been physically chastised by their stepfather. The boys had marks on them and both seemed upset by the way they were treated by the stepfather. The referral report stated that both children expressed dislike for the stepfather. The child-protection investigation concluded that the stepfather did not take the professionals' concerns about his treatment of the boys seriously or implied that it was an appropriate way of disciplining the boys when they misbehaved. The mother was then given an ultimatum that unless the stepfather left the home the children would be removed from her care. The parents decided to split up and the stepfather left the family.

When I saw the family the mother was a bit bewildered by what had happened. She was guarded and almost suspicious about the whole process of assessment, let alone the idea of 'help'. She expressed some feelings of helplessness about what had happened. The two boys were well behaved and also very guarded; they sat in their chairs looking watchful but not playing with the toy materials. The history was that the mother's first marriage to the boys' father had broken down and he had returned to live in Pakistan; there was no contact with him. She married the stepfather, in

Britain, and had another child by him. The marriage became strained, as her own family who were in Britain did not approve of the new husband and rejected both her and the family. The two boys had difficulty accepting him, and became quite disobedient and difficult to manage. The mother said she regretted that all these pressures had led to the break-up of the family. She seemed quite sad and distressed to think that if they had had more support from their families things might have turned out better. She realized that the stepfather might wish to maintain contact with the youngest, his own child, but she seemed pessimistic, in the light of what had happened, that this would be possible. The boys could not talk openly, if at all, about their experiences with the stepfather in such a tense and uneasy atmosphere. The mother turned down the offer of therapeutic help or support for the family. This was hardly surprising following her experience of professional or outside intervention.

Hodes (1992) pointed out that the variations in child-rearing practices make a universal definition of 'child abuse' difficult if not impossible. He suggests that professionals, when faced with the task of assessing a particular practice, should determine if it fits into one of three categories: first, a practice which represents cultural variation in parenting practices; second, a practice which represents an idiosyncratic departure from societal norms of behaviour; third, if it is a case where there is societal harm to children in cases of famine or war – this is particularly relevant in working with refugee families.

DIFFERENT FAMILY STRUCTURES

The relationship between family structure, social organization and culture is complex and not clearly understood. There is an inherent danger in viewing the different types of behaviour in a family as expressions of the rules within their ethnic group (Perelberg, 1992). To do so would be a failure to take into account the wide variations within cultures or ethnic groups. Lau (1984) described two types of family structure which do not conform to Western norms: the single parent in Afro-Caribbean families, and the extended family groups in one household in Asian families. Vyas (1991) described the typical Asian family unit or household as comprising three generations with paternal grandparents, married sons and their families, unmarried sons, and occasionally uncles and widowed daughters.

'Culture' has been defined as a system of rules which governs behaviour, a system of beliefs (McGoldrick, 1982). It has also been defined as a 'web of meaning' (Geertz, 1972). Perelberg (1992) warned against perceiving cultures in general terms, as if they were monolithic entities, e.g. the Asian or Afro-Caribbean. She believes that it is important, when one is dealing with families from ethnic minorities in a Western context, to keep in mind that these are families who have embarked on a process of ethnic redefinition which entails the creation of new arrangements which are different from those prevailing in their original home setting and from those in their new environment.

Case example 3: an African girl

The family referred consisted of an African father, an English mother, their three young sons, and the father's two younger teenage sisters. The father's younger sister was stealing from her peers at school, from shops, and from the family at home. The referral came at the instigation of the mother who saw the girl's behaviour as an indication that she might be depressed or unhappy. The father was sceptical about the referral and the idea of getting psychological help. He saw the behaviour as an anti-social act which needed strict disciplinary measures, and the stealing as simply opportunist.

I initially tried to get the parents to agree on a management strategy, to closely supervise her and, using a behavioural strategy, reward her when she was not stealing. This was unsuccessful. During the sessions we further explored each of the parents' beliefs and ideas about the problems. The mother thought that the girl's behaviour reflected her unhappiness at not having her own mother, someone she felt close to and could confide in. She was critical of her husband for not making the time to talk to his sister or help her confide in him. The father thought that the sister received enough attention from adults and in fact far more than she would have got had she stayed on in Africa with their family. He thought that she would talk to or confide in older sisters or her peers, and did not think it was appropriate for him to try to spend time with her.

What emerged were two different systems of beliefs, meanings and explanatory models. It seems that the family's own culture was in a state of evolution, as the couple struggled to integrate the two cultures, Western and African. Positively reframing the girl's behaviour as her way of helping them in that process of clarification and or in reaching an agreement was moderately successful.

Lau (1984) sees important differences between non-western extended family systems and western nuclear family systems. She describes the former as one where breaks are not expected between generations and continuity in the group depends on the presence of three generations. The old are necessary in order to provide a complete model of life and central authority figures. The family group is governed by the principle of interdependence and constitutes the most important unit in society. This is contrasted to the Western nuclear family culture where the individual constitutes the most important unit, and self-sufficiency and personal autonomy are highly valued. There are important clinical implications for this. Hodes (1989) suggests that the professional should assume that older family members, e.g. grandparents, will have greater authority. Lau (1984) thinks it is important when working with such families to look at key relationships and boundaries in a different way. There are several important clinical considerations which follow from such ideas, such as the appropriateness of always expecting to interview the whole family. The expectation on the part of professionals to have members of the family speaking openly in the presence of an outsider, especially for children to speak freely about and in front of their parents, transgresses intergenerational and cultural rules about communications. Harris (1994) suggests meeting with parts of the family, at least to begin with, could be more productive, e.g. meeting the parents on their own first, then with the referred child.

Case example 4: an Indian Sikh family

The Suallys, an Indian Sikh family, was referred because of various professionals' concerns about several of the children in the family. The oldest daughter who was nineteen had a serious psychiatric disorder, the third oldest daughter who was sixteen had difficulty with school attendance and was exhibiting odd and anti-social behaviour, the ten-year-old son was refusing to attend school.

Without going into too much detail of a long and complicated family history, it can be said that most professionals who had tried to work with the family felt frustrated at what was felt to be the parents' inability or reluctance to discuss openly their apparent conflicts and/or disagreement about managing things within the family. They noticed how the mother would only talk about disagreements with her husband in his absence and when seen on her own. These included his occasional violence towards her, or his 'too close' relationship with his own parents. The father too seemed critical of his wife as a mother, but would not discuss this in her presence. When both parents were seen with the grandparents, again father deferred to his own father to answer questions about the children while the mother would be completely silent and could not be drawn to express any of her concerns regarding what she had previously confided, her feeling of being undermined by her in-laws.

I initially started seeing the couple together with various combinations of the children and encountered the same difficulty. It was difficult not to come to the same conclusion about the distorted pattern of communications in the family and to see it as responsible for their difficulties. This is of course partly true. The problem remained that the family did not or could not engage with professionals who tried to help and they continued to have serious problems. I then started to see different parts of the family, i.e. the father on his own who, interestingly, suggested that I speak with his wife on her own, which I did with the help of an interpreter. During the interviews they openly discussed their concerns about the other and asked me on their behalf to explain this to the other. I also discovered from talking to the father that he would often ask another senior female in the extended family or their social network to explain things to his wife, for example the importance of taking her medication. (Mrs Sually was diabetic.)

I think I was able to engage the parents by recognizing and accepting rather than confronting or challenging the cultural rules about communication within the family. I am still working with the family, hoping to empower the parents to find their own way to help their children.

PROVIDING A CULTURALLY SENSITIVE SERVICE

In my experience professionals need to give some thought to the way services are delivered or provided as well as to their practice when considering the needs of people from non-Western ethnic minorities. To begin with, it would be important to get the basic information about the ethnic groups in their area, what religions they practise and which languages they speak. Considering the under-utilization of child mental health services and psychological services in general, some ethnic monitoring or auditing of referrals or uptake of services is a good way to start. Employing link workers or cultural go-betweens is a useful way of raising awareness and combating racist attitudes.

A service model which offers initial home-based assessments and therapeutic work when appropriate, or less reliance on institutional care, is more likely to be sensitive to the needs of families from minorities who feel apprehensive or reluctant to come forward for help. In my experience, large sections of ethnic minorities are made up of families with young children under five or of primary school age. The mothers, who usually have the primary responsibility for the care of the children, have great difficulty travelling with children to attend appointments. Home visits would make the service more accessible to them and help them overcome their uneasiness about coming forward for help. I found it very instructive to see the family living conditions. Therapeutic intervention needs to be about housing, economic deprivation, dealing with racism. It needs to take into account the children and their families' actual and real needs rather than any theoretical formulation.

THE THERAPEUTIC ENCOUNTER

Any encounter between a professional and the family with a child who has an emotional problem is a meeting between two cultures – the therapist's and the family's. This is more evident with families from ethnic minorities. The meeting contains a conflict between potentially opposing views of childhood, of family life and of the world.

Boyd-Franklin (1989) and O'Brien (1990) both emphasize that at their first encounter with families from ethnic minorities, professionals need to recognize that the families will see them first and foremost as agents of institutions which they perceive or experience as prejudiced or racist. Therefore there is great need to be respectful of the family's beliefs and views and their own explanatory model for the problem.

Case example 5: first-generation-English Hindu children

Nicky, who was 17, referred himself because he was feeling very anxious about his forthcoming exams. He is the second in a family of three children; the family are Hindu from India, but the children were all born in England.

At the first interview mother and the three children came. The mother spoke at length about her worries and struggles to bring up the children almost on her own after the break-up of her marriage. She was tearful at times, but whenever I or my co-therapist interrupted to sympathize, she seemed irritated and not really comforted by our comments; it felt as if she felt patronized. We could clearly see that Nicky was a very able student; he had already been offered a place at university, the other two children were doing very well academically. However, the mother went on to complain about Nicky being lazy and not concentrating. We wondered whether she was depressed and suggested that she might need treatment herself. Again her reaction was the same. As the interview progressed, and at subsequent interviews, we realized that what the mother really wanted from us was to listen respectfully to her instead of repeatedly telling her 'we know what it must have been like'. Of course we did not, particularly about the amount of prejudice and racism that she endured, some of it at the hands of professionals like ourselves.

So far, we had responded to her distress or request for help in a similar manner. We recognized that this kind of misunderstanding is common with professionals like us when we try to impose our own views or values. The mother did not expect sympathy or praise from us, nor did she see herself as sacrificing her life for the children. This was her expectation of herself and it was what was expected of her. This clash or conflict between two cultures or ideas about family life was more clearly illustrated at a later interview. The mother talked about how she was looking forward to the time when all her children would have completed their education and were established independently. In response one of us said, 'You must be looking forward to having some time for yourself' to which she replied, 'No, I am hoping to go home to India and give some time to my mother'.

This case taught us to be careful about our own assumptions, and to enquire respectfully from families about their views and beliefs before giving advice. As the mother felt listened-to and realized that her concerns were being taken seriously, she felt empowered and supported to help and reassure her son who was really doing very well. He went on to pass his exams with flying colours.

LANGUAGE AND USING INTERPRETERS

For many families from non-Western ethnic minorities, the most fluent English-speakers, may be the youngest members. If English is the only language, or if the children are being used to interpret, this could lead to a reversal of the traditional hierarchy and organization. The parents might feel ashamed and embarrassed because of their lack of fluency. It is more appropriate to use adult interpreters. This will convey an important message to the parents that the helper is interested in and values their views. There are special problems that arise when using interpreters. The unsophisticated interpreter might not be able to translate the subtle communication or what the family means by what they say. An interpreter cannot always help to identify the uniqueness of the family's idioms and metaphors. Interpreters should not be used as a conduit for the professional's ideas. I have found it useful to meet with the interpreter beforehand to explain what I am trying to do and find out his or her ideas about the family. It is more helpful to have continuity by using the same interpreter with the same family. Ideally a service should have access to a group of interpreters in the relevant languages, who could be included in the community-based multi-disciplinary team.

Case example 6: a Chinese family's communication difficulties

The Chan family's oldest son Ray was admitted to the local in-patient adolescent unit with a diagnosis of obsessive-compulsive disorder. He had been hoarding rubbish in his bedroom, refused to have a bath or cut his nails or his hair.

I worked with the family with the help of a Chinese interpreter. After several months and numerous interviews, I realized that we had made little headway. The parents remained courteous and friendly, but we both realized that we were not getting through to each other. Often the parents did not or could not implement a management strategy or carry out a home-based task which I had thought they had agreed to in a previous session. I was left puzzled and frustrated, and they felt hopeless at the lack of progress. I had been meeting the interpreter only during the interview, and he always left with the family; we had no contact between sessions.

I then decided to meet the interpreter on his own and discuss the situation. I was very interested to learn from him that he found it very difficult to interpret my suggestions or directions to the family. This was partly linguistic but also cultural. For example, he felt it was at odds with cultural norms to talk about an adolescent leaving home or going to live in a hostel. He thought it would be quite inappropriate to expect the parents to talk openly about their adolescent son going to live elsewhere with mere strangers. This would be seen as shameful. So it emerged that he had found it very difficult to convey my ideas to the parents, especially as he was not really clear about what I was trying to do. So in fact, most of the time he was telling the parents what he thought I ought to say or what would be more acceptable culturally. We were able to clarify each other's views and he helped me make some sense of the parents' views and behaviour when they did not comply with agreed (as I had thought) strategies.

At a later session I was joined by a Chinese-speaking therapist colleague, and I was not surprised to discover that I had completely confused the parents' positions in relation to Ray's problems. This was a turning point in the work with the family, we were able to set more realistic tasks for them and work toward goals that were more acceptable or congruent with their own values and beliefs.

GENDER, AGE, RACE

There are certain attributes of the therapist/professional which will be significant to the family, such as age and gender. In non-Western cultures increasing age and maleness are associated with increasing authority.

However, for certain families the therapist's role, regardless of attributes, will be invested with much authority. What matters in working with children and their families is that professionals need to be aware of and give thought to these issues. Another issue is the race or ethnicity of the therapist. I have already stated the importance for the therapist at the beginning of the contact to have racism on the agenda. Only when it is spoken about openly with the child and the family would they be able to raise it as an issue. I think there is a paradox for white therapists raising the issue of racism; it is different with black or non-white therapists. There is an assumption that therapists are more likely to engage and have greater understanding or empathy with families from similar cultural or ethnic background. There is an argument for 'matching' of the therapist's race or ethnicity with that of the family as a way of tackling racism. This is what DiNicola (1985) called the 'insider' perspective. Hodes (1989) has, however, pointed out that racial matching has many disadvantages. First, there is a tendency to confuse race and culture. Secondly, the cultures of ethnic minorities are changing, so in reality people do not come from discrete ethnic groups with rigid boundaries. For Hodes (1989) the skill of the informed therapist is to use his difference to his or her advantage from the 'outsider' perspective. I believe, in the end, that what matters is that the therapist should respectfully enquire about the family's rituals and seek to find their views. Vyas (1991) asserts that sensitivity and culturally acceptable interventions are more important than the 'right cultural mix' between therapist and family.

THERAPEUTIC INTERVENTIONS

I would like to consider briefly the issue of the relationship between the type of therapy and the culture of the family. It is possible that there is a fit between certain types of therapeutic intervention and the culture of the child and the family. In my experience, in non-Western cultures and societies where the family is very central, individual psychotherapy is less acceptable (Neki *et al.*, 1985). Vyas (1991) suggests that task-setting and behavioural focal therapy are better understood by Asian families than insight-giving therapy. Messent (1992) suggests that Bangladeshi families prefer structured, goal-directed work with clear and concrete realistic objectives. In all societies, but especially non-Western societies, professionals (e.g. doctors, teachers or therapists) are held in high esteem and are expected to provide answers and prescriptions. There is reluctance among professionals in the mental health fields, and psychotherapists in general, to offer direct advice or an opinion. This 'neutral' stance is in conflict with the expectations in cultures where emotional or psychological problems are usually understood in terms of laziness, or as being influenced by bad 'spirits', 'Ginns' or the 'evil eye'. Therefore it is expected that help could take the form of a 'pep talk' from the physician, elder, priest or Imam. Messent (1992) refers to the therapist being seen as a knowledgeable expert who is expected to give advice and direction. It is advisable during the early stages of the therapeutic work to avoid detailed taking of history or gathering of information. Rack (1982) suggests this is likely to be experienced as intrusive, given ethnic minority family experiences of some institutions such as the immigration department.

Sluzki (1979) stressed the need for the therapist to pay attention to the different phases that families pass through in the process of migration to a new country, and advised that different help forms may be appropriate for each phase. Ho (1987) suggests that requests for help from recently arrived immigrant families are likely to be for information, advocacy and concrete services, and that such requests should be responded to as a way of gaining the family's trust.

In my practice I do write letters to the housing department or to the social security department to help them with their benefits. Another common request is from parents asking for further or more medical tests for the referred child, such as X-ray, EEG. I often respond to these requests by making the appropriate referrals to other specialists. I think it is important to recognize the relative power and authority which the therapist/helper or expert has, and to be prepared to use it on behalf of the family to gain their confidence before any therapy can take place. Finally, it is very useful as Lau (1984) pointed out to re-frame whenever possible the identified child's problem behaviour as a normal response to the family worries. Bott and Hodes (1989) found that structural family therapy, which focuses on issues of authority, boundaries and rules, is more suitable for non-individualistic societies, (for example African ones) which are quite hierarchical and where the individual is constituted through the kinship group.

SUMMARY

I have given an overview of the theoretical and clinical issues relevant to working with children and their families from non-Western ethnic minorities. I would caution against hasty generalizations and suggest proper regard be given to the sociocultural background of each family. My comments and suggestions regarding clinical practice can be seen to apply to working with families from all cultural backgrounds or, really, to be about general good practice. Still, I do think they are even more relevant in working with children from non-Western cultural backgrounds.

REFERENCES

Ballard, R. and Ballard, C. (1977) The Sikhs: the development of South Asian settlements in Britain. In J. Watson (ed.) *Between Cultures*, Oxford: Blackwell, pp. 21–56.

Bott, D. and Hodes, M. (1989) Structural family therapy for a West African family. *Journal of Family Therapy*, **11**, 169–79.

Boyd-Franklin, N. (1989) *Black Families In Therapy: A Multi-systems Approach*. New York: Syracuse University Press.

DiNicola, V.F. (1985) Family therapy and transcultural psychiatry: an emerging synthesis. *Transcultural Psychiatric Research Review*, **22**, 81–113; 151–81.

EL-Hadi, A. (1993) Administrative outcome of referrals of families from non-Western background to the Child and Family Consultation Centre, Redbridge. Unpublished audit presentation at King George Hospital, Redbridge.

Fernando, S. (1991) *Mental Health, Race and Culture*. New York: Mind Publications.

Geertz, C. (1972) *The Interpretation of Cultures*. New York: Basic Books.

Gibbs, T., Huang, L.N. *et al.* (1989) *Children of Colour: Psychological Intervention with Minority Youth*. San Francisco: Jossey-Bass.

Harris, Q. (1994) A systemic approach to working with families from ethnic minority background. *Context News Magazine of Family Therapy*, **20**, 31–7.

Ho, M.K.H. (1987) *Family Therapy with Ethnic Minorities*. London: Sage.

Hodes, M. (1989) Annotation: culture and family therapy. *Journal of Family Therapy*, **11**, 117–28.

Hodes, M. (1992) The clinical relevance of the social anthropology of childhood. *Newsletter of the Association of Child Psychology and Psychiatry*, **14**, 257–62.

Kallarckal, A. and Herbert, M. (1976) The happiness of Indian immigrant children. *New Society*, **4**, 22–4.

Kleinman, A. and Good, B. (eds) (1985) *Culture and Depression: Studies in the Anthropology of Cross Cultural Psychiatry of Affects and Mood Disorder*. Berkeley, California: University of California Press.

Lau, A. (1984) Transcultural issues in family therapy. *Journal of Family Therapy*, **6**, 91–112.

Littlewood, R. (1992) DSM-IV and culture: is the classification internationally valid? *Psychiatric Bulletin*, **16**, 257–61.

Littlewood, R. and Lipsege, M. (1987) The butterfly and the serpent: culture, psycho-pathology and biomedicine. *Cultural, Medicine and Psychiatry*, **11**, 289–335.

McGoldrick, M., Pearce, J. and Giardino, R. (eds) (1982) *Ethnicity and Family Therapy*. New York: Guildford Press.

Messent, P. (1992) Working with Bangladeshi families in the East end of London. *Journal of Family Therapy*, **14**, 287–304.

Neki, J.S., Joint, B. *et al.* (1985) The cultural perspective of therapeutic relationships, a point of view from Africa. *Acta Psychiatrica Scandinavica*, **71**, 543–50.

Newth, S. (1986) Emotional and behavioural disorders in the children of Asian immigrants. *Newsletter of the Association of Child Psychology and Psychiatry*, **8**, 10–14.

O'Brien, C. (1990) Family therapy and black families. *Journal of Family Therapy*, **12**, 3–16.

Perelberg, R. (1992) Familiar and unfamiliar types of family structure. In J. Kareem and R. Littlewood (eds) *Intercultural Therapy: Themes, Interpretation and Practice*. Oxford: Blackwell Scientific.

Rack, P. (1982) *Race, Culture, and Mental Disorder*. London: Tavistock.

Sluzki, G. (1979) Migration and family conflict. *Family Process*, **18**, 379–90.

Stern, G., Cotterol, D. and Holmes, J. (1990) Patterns of attendance of child psychiatry out-patients with special reference to Asian children. *British Journal of Psychiatry*, **156**, 384–7.

Vyas, I. (1991) Emotional problems of Asian children: a practical guide. *Newsletter of the Association of Child Psychology and Psychiatry*, **13**, 10–15.

CHAPTER 9

Helping the Families of Problem Children

K. Eia Asen

PROBLEM CHILDREN AND THEIR LIVING CONTEXTS

The term 'problem child' has, of course, no place in any formal psychiatric classification systems. Nevertheless it has become a kind of accepted short-hand for children who cause considerable worries to their parents and others, be they tedious toddlers, depressed teenagers or delinquent adolescents. The specific root causes of such problem behaviours stem from a wide variety of factors: genes, constitution, social factors, physical illness, family dynamics, unsuitable friends, school, etc. This chapter looks at how the family may contribute to the emergence of a problem child, how problem children can contribute to a family becoming a 'problem family' and how families with problem children can be helped.

The vast majority of 'problem children' are not born with problems as such, but generally acquire these in the process of growing up. The family provides the setting within which problems develop and specific family dynamics can play a major role. At what point a certain child is defined as a 'problem child' can vary a great deal: what is a problem child to one family may well be a normal one to another. It very much depends on who makes the 'diagnosis'. Problems manifest themselves in different contexts, such as the home, school or neighbourhood. And it very much depends on the 'norms' of these very contexts as to when, how and why a child gets labelled as a 'problem'.

Different families and different (sub-)cultures can have widely divergent views concerning which behaviours are problematic. For example, the adolescent daughter of a first-generation immigrant Bengali family who answers back and stays out until the early hours of the morning may well be regarded by her parents as a 'problem child'. Yet her behaviour may be seen as entirely 'normal' by her Western(ized) peer group and their respective parents. These cannot see anything wrong with what they regard as the girl's 'typical adolescent behaviour'. At the same time the Bengali parents are desperate to get outside help so that their daughter can again learn to respect her parents and their culturally-determined expectations and values.

Even within the same culture, however, there may be considerable variation in what is defined as normal and what is problematic. The enuretic 9-year-old who grows up in a family where no other members have been dry before their early teens will appear 'normal' in his family, whereas he or she may be a 'problem child' to the school doctor and other professionals who, statistically speaking, expect children to be dry much earlier. In another case, a shy and friendless 12-year-old girl may be 'a perfectly normal child' to her antisocial parents, but is seen as a 'problem child' by her grandparents who cannot help but see family history repeating itself: this, after all, seems to be the way things started with *their* offspring . . .

Family dynamics can clearly be a major force in contributing to a child's becoming defined as a problem, and this is particularly evident when there is constant overt disagreement between both parents as to whether their son or daughter is a 'problem child' or not. Such disagreements often have a complex background and may be a way of settling old scores, but if children get caught between their parents they can develop a very confused sense of self. Figure 9.1 illustrates more formally the various contexts that surround a child.

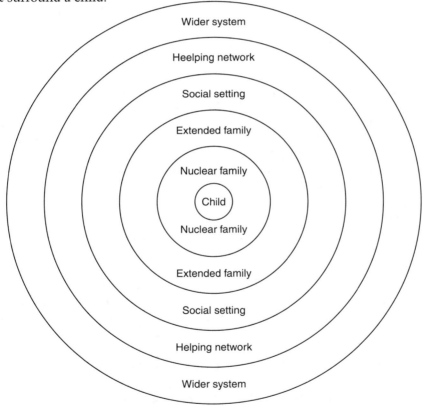

Figure 9.1. Contexts surrounding the child

The idea that problem behaviours can be viewed as being, at least in part, context-determined has a number of implications for clinical practice. The clinician will wish to establish how, when and where problem children are 'a problem' and how these problems may fluctuate depending on the various contexts within which the child operates. More specifically, the following questions need to be raised and answered during the assessment:

- *Who* is this child a problem to? – mother, father, both parents, the school? Who is this child *not* a problem to?
- *Why now?* Why not before? Why not later? What is going on in the family/school now which has caused the problem child to be referred?
- *Where?* Where do the problems manifest themselves? Who is around? Who makes the problems better or worse? Where and when is the problem child *not* a problem?
- *How?* How do these problems manifest themselves? How do they evolve? What is actually happening?

It will not be possible to find answers to these questions merely by examining the child. It is necessary to involve other people from the child's living contexts, above all the parents and other important family members, teachers and, if relevant, other professionals involved in caring for the child and family. The aim is to map out how the problem behaviours fluctuate in different contexts and how the different contexts and persons may affect the behaviours of the problem child.

Let us look at an example to illustrate how the problem child may present in different contexts. Jimmy, an Afro-Caribbean boy aged 12, is aggressive to his little sister. His single mother sees him as a problem child, reminding her of his father. The grandparents regard Jimmy as normal: 'All boys are like that, they are just more boisterous'. Jimmy's school, a large inner-London comprehensive, finds his aggressive behaviour 'normal' compared with that of his peer group. The workers at the youth club, however, see him as disruptive and call him a 'problem child'. The neighbours on the housing estate find Jimmy 'polite and quiet'. The GP (male), approached by Jimmy's mother, confirms the 'problem child' diagnosis. The social worker, whom mother involves after Jimmy stayed out very late following some arguments at home, believes that mother is too preoccupied with Jimmy's younger sister and believes 'mother is the problem'. When an elderly woman is mugged by a gang of teenagers on Jimmy's estate, the local press writes about 'black problem children' and the local newspaper shop promptly bans Jimmy from buying sweets: 'I know all about you problem kids'.

We can see from this example that the very same child's behaviour can be perceived very differently by different people and agencies. Moreover, Jimmy may behave quite differently in different settings and in the presence of different people. The point is that problems are partially social constructions; they are certainly not fixed entities which are part of the make-up of a child – they are dynamic, not static.

How the problem is defined very much determines the 'site' for intervention, be it the family, the school or the problem child. Moreover, the professional's own working context will also very much define what is to be done, if anything. Child psychiatrists, health visitors and social workers (who are all concerned with child protection) tend to focus predominantly on the welfare of the child and are thus more inclined to take the side of children, seeing them as the victims of inadequate parenting. Adult psychiatrists and allied workers tend to take a somewhat different perspective and think more about how best to ease the parental burden. It is not uncommon for there to be competing views on how to help parents manage a problem child. This is related to the different positions professionals occupy in the helping network and it can lead to conflict between the various agencies. If there are a number of professionals involved then it is important to convene a network meeting so that professionals and parents can coordinate their efforts and work with rather than against one another.

PROBLEM CHILDREN, FAMILY MYTHS AND FAMILY SCRIPTS

Problems are often connected with belief systems that families have developed over many years. Whether they are consciously aware of it or not, most families have their own scripts, organized by myths or fixed beliefs about what is right or wrong, who is like whom, the 'traditional' roles of men and women, and so on. Some of these beliefs are openly stated and others are never talked about. When such beliefs are acted upon we can talk about a family script – and all families have such scripts, usually perfected over generations, transmitted from one generation to the next. Each successive generation may adopt a similar approach to life and thereby replicate the script. Alternatively, in order to avoid their parents' mistakes, the next generation may re-write or correct the familiar script (Byng-Hall, 1985). For example, if one felt ignored and neglected as a child one might try to give one's offspring as much love as possible. But an 'overdose' of mothering (or fathering) can stifle the child's emotional growth. Soon we have what many people might regard as a problem child who presents as over-dependent, unable to separate, anxious and with poor social skills.

Family myths can be powerful and re-awaken old ghosts. One father told the story of how he 'knew' that his little Jane was not normal the moment she was born. She reminded him so much of his sister who developed schizophrenia in her late teens. Ever since Jane's infancy he had looked closely for similarities between her and his sister – and 'found' them. When Jane was 12 years old her father was convinced that she would sooner or later have a 'nervous breakdown'. Jane herself had of course been indirectly aware of her father's worries although the question of schizophrenia had never been openly discussed. She knew that her father thought that there was something wrong with her, but had been unable to figure out what this was. It made her start doubting her own sanity.

If fears or expectations are projected upon children it can become a big burden for them. If this goes on for long enough the result may well be that a child eventually 'accepts' such projections and ends up by performing the role imposed. The power of such myths and scripts in creating a problem child cannot be underestimated, particularly if they involve an already sensitive or vulnerable child. Parents are often unaware that their (well meant) concerns and anxieties can act as self-fulfilling prophecies and significantly contribute to the emergence of a problem child.

Apart from family myths there are many other family dynamics which can enhance a child's vulnerability and lead to a presentation of a problem child. Parental depression can be another huge burden for children. It often leaves them emotionally neglected so that they become depressed themselves and usually present in school as shy and withdrawn. However, there are children who grow up with a depressed parent but go to another extreme. In their wish to cheer up the parent they may become 'over-active', restless and disruptive.

Many problem children come from what people call 'unhappy homes'. Serious marital discord, with violence between the parents, can force children from an early age to arbitrate or become a go-between, – and then become symptomatic themselves. Some children, in their conscious or unconscious efforts to save their parents' marriage, may go to extremes and play up every time the temperature between the parents is raised. The child may shout, scream and kick louder than the parents. This is very likely to distract the parents from their own battle and they join forces, temporarily, to get their 'naughty' son or daughter under control. The parents' battle is thus stopped and their frustrations are taken out on the child. In this way children learn to 'sacrifice' themselves to restore or preserve the peace between the parents, often without consciously planning to do so.

Sexually-abused children who have been threatened and sworn to secrecy can indirectly communicate their distress by presenting as 'problem children'. Self-mutilating teenagers, for example, draw attention to physical wounds which are the concrete representation of invisible injuries inflicted on them, often over a long period of time. It may take them years to reveal the causes for their distress directly.

Unresolved bereavement issues can present themselves through a problem child who may unwittingly 'impersonate' in speech, posture and other behaviours a deceased grandparent or other relative. The family frequently fails to make such connections and merely sees the young person as 'bizarre', if not 'crazy'. In this way the child fills a space vacated by an important family member whose death cannot be talked about.

CONVENING FAMILY MEETINGS

When asked to see a problem child, most clinicians will first think about how to involve the parents and other family members in the therapeutic work. *Not* involving the parents from the outset is now thankfully the exception rather than the rule. There need to be clear and convincing reasons as to why the family should not participate in the therapeutic work with their problem child. Not infrequently parents prefer to hand over the problem to someone else, such as a child psychiatrist, psychologist or social worker: *'You* sort him out!' can be a very understandable request, but if responded to automatically it deprives the parents and other family members of participating, at least initially, in the therapeutic process. The child at a later stage may require individual help; but, if he or she is plugged into an expert too soon, this can inhibit the family from using and developing its own knowledge and expertise.

As many parents cannot help blaming themselves (or each other) for their children's problems, it is very important that the first meetings are set up sensitively. Parents can feel quite alarmed by the suggestion that the whole family should attend. If the somewhat unfortunate term 'family therapy' is mentioned prior to such a first family meeting, then the whole venture may be off to a bad start. Many parents do not take kindly to the notion that their family requires 'therapy', and see the very notion of 'family therapy' as an assault on their togetherness and well-meaning hard work. In practice it may be useful to offer a less alarming formula, namely convening 'family meetings' and explaining that it would be useful to have the whole family present at the first meeting so that everyone's view of the problem (child) can be taken into account. It could be added that it helps to see how each person is affected by the problem (child) and how their responses, in turn, affect the problem (child). In this way the family becomes a resource, joining with the clinician to help the problem child.

During the initial stages of family work, the focus is therefore on the child's problem behaviour: when and how it occurs, when it is better and when it is worse, who can influence it, and if so, in what direction and so on. The aim is to understand what all the real or perceived problems are, who sees what as problems and who not, and to chart how the problem behaviours fluctuate. This will lead to the formulation of working hypotheses about why behaviours are present and why they vary according to context. But apart from helping to generate hypotheses, these questions are interventions in their own right: they set a process in motion whereby all family members get slowly involved in questioning their own and other family members' assumptions and habitual responses.

This form of interventive questioning has its root in the techniques of 'circular questioning' (Palazzoli *et al.*, 1980). The clinician conducts the interview by seeking information about how each person views problems, relationships and certain events. As different persons may have quite different perceptions about these, such a style of interviewing will bring out differences. Not infrequently family members are surprised or puzzled by some of the answers they hear from their nearest and dearest. This leads to family members questioning or contradicting one another directly, and raising points which have often never been raised. The recognition that different family members entertain quite different ideas about certain issues can be quite perturbing to certain families. The questions stimulate family interaction and self-reflection; bring disagreements out into the open; and everyone's thinking is set in motion, one hopes along an unfamiliar path. The clinician responds to the family's feedback by highlighting the very different ways people answer the same question. In this way the clinician acts as a catalyst, making possible certain reactions and interactions that might otherwise not happen. In this way assumptions may be challenged, old beliefs questioned and secrets opened up.

The process of questioning aims to get the family and its members to look at themselves in a new light. It has the effect of getting people to reflect about some of their fixed beliefs. Above all it tends to shake the belief that all the problems are located in the problem child. Often people discover that it might be 'convenient' to identify one person as 'the problem' rather than looking at their own contribution. The timing of this type of questioning is crucial: challenging a family in the first family meetings can have adverse consequences. If the family as a whole or certain individuals feel threatened, they are likely to 'fire' the clinician and not return for their next appointment.

When working with families it is vital to 'join' (Minuchin, 1974) with each family member, forming therapeutic alliances as it were. Every person in the family needs to know that the clinician is in tune with them, that their specific position is understood and respected. A good clinician is able to have multiple perspectives and knows that there is not just one valid view or just one truth. If a member of the family perceives the clinician to be against them, it is difficult to work together for the welfare of the child. It can cause problems, not just for the clinician, but for different family members, including the problem child. The parents may even blame the problem child for having behaved so 'reasonably' in the presence of the clinician and he or she may be punished for good behaviour.

At the end of the first meeting with the family, the clinician hopes that the parents will leave feeling that they are not being blamed for their child's problems, but with the hope that they can contribute something positive so that their child can recover. Similarly the problem child should not leave feeling singled-out as the person who causes such terrible worry to the parents. Instead, he or she should feel like part of a family which is very much trying to help.

It is in the following family meetings that addressing the problems within a family context takes place. Generally speaking, at the outset of family work the focus will be on the presenting problem(s) (Asen and Tomson 1992). Even if it appears that the parents are at the root of the problem it is usually unwise to confront them or relate the child's problem behaviour to issues within the marriage. The parents are likely to deny this and family work will get off on the wrong footing, with the parents in opposition to the clinician. It is only at the point when the problem behaviour changes that the family is likely to look at some of the more long-term family issues – such as myths, secrets, alliances and scapegoating. It is in the middle phase of family work that historical issues can be explored, examining the past with reference to present relationship issues and long-established family patterns. The last phase of family work is usually concerned with relapse prevention: identifying the warning signs and considering what evasive action to take, how to not allow the home situation to get too bad, and how to build on successes.

CASE EXAMPLES OF PROBLEM CHILDREN

This section illustrates the application of family therapy ideas and techniques to managing problem children of different ages. A few specific examples are described, but many of the techniques used are also applicable to other problems or age groups.

Taming out-of-control toddlers

Children who are prone to excessive temper tantrums can be extremely taxing to their parents. Screaming matches can last for hours and if these are accompanied by kicking, biting and scratching, then the parents can get out of control themselves. Physical confrontations can and do result in the child being hurt. Many non-accidental injuries are not the result of sadistic parents deliberately inflicting injuries on their children. Instead they can be seen as the consequence of parents not intervening at the outset and allowing an escalation to occur. At some point these parents can no longer think of how to stop the battle, and this is when they resort to physical means which can get seriously out of hand. Characteristically, many of the children who are regarded by their parents as 'little monsters' are as good as gold in other settings, the nursery for example. This is doubly infuriating to the parents, who cannot help but think that the child is deliberately winding them up, and this makes it even more likely that the parents will lose control.

With smaller children who present with tantrums or control issues, part of the assessment is to see what happens when the child produces the problem behaviour. Seeing this happen in the consulting room can provide a unique opportunity to study the family's interactions around the problem behaviour and thus inform alternative strategies. Unfortunately, many children do not spontaneously produce the problem behaviours the first time they meet the clinician; they tend to be on best behaviour, having been warned by their parents prior to the consultation. Parents are of course in two minds as to whether the clinician should see what they have to cope with. On the one hand it would help, but at the same time they might feel publicly shamed if the child 'threw a wobbly'. It is for this reason that the clinician might ask the family to 'enact the problem' (Minuchin, 1974). This can be done by means of a fairly simple formula, namely asking the parent(s) the following question: 'What is it that you would have to say or do now for your child to produce the sort of problems that have brought you here?' This question encourages parents to think about trigger points.

Most parents know what to do or say, whether this means asking the child to sit down on a chair, put the toys away or play with little sister. Soon an enactment takes place, with the child resisting the parental instructions, the parent or parents getting slowly more and more cross, the child escalating further and the parents coming close to explosion point. It is at this juncture that many parents give in or up, and this results in the child winning – once again. It is now the clinician's task to point out how the little child is defeating the parents. The likely consequences of the child running his or her own show must then be discussed. Parents are encouraged to weigh up the pros and cons of continuing the battle. The clinician's aim is to keep up the pressure on the parents to find a new resolution to an all-too-familiar problem. This can induce a quasi-therapeutic crisis which pushes the situation beyond its normal limits, particularly if the parents are discouraged from resorting to the use of smacking or other forms of physical punishment. Sitting it out can have miraculous effects, but this usually requires a lot of resolve on the parents' part; they might just about be able to maintain this with the clinician's support. The little 'monster' is unlikely to give up the advantage he or she has gained over months, if not years. It requires the parents' full commitment to see it through in order to ensure that the child gets the message that it is the parents who call the shots. It may take one hour to 'tame the monster' and it needs to be followed up by many more 'rounds' at home so that the child realizes that the parents have joined forces and are determined to win – without physical or emotional hurt. The family meeting is not finished before the parents have achieved control. What started out as an assessment has become a therapeutic session with a positive outcome: the parent has achieved something that has not been achieved hitherto. Getting the parents to be and remain in charge of their child also helps them to remain in charge of their own responses and this is therefore one good step towards preventing child abuse.

The technique of 'enactment' makes the problems and responses come alive in the room and these can be studied at the time or, if necessary, afterwards with the parents through video play-back: this makes it possible to observe in minute detail how problems get triggered, how they escalate and how they might be resolved in different ways. Pausing a video sequence from time to time allows parents to reflect on different endings which the familiar scripts could have. It makes it possible to identify alternative strategies and to discuss, from a different perspective and with a cool head, what could be done differently the next time a similar scenario arises. Moreover, there is an important message in the fact that the parents were able to get the enactment going in the first place. If parents know how to 'turn on' a tantrum then it might be equally possible to switch one off. In fact, it is the recognition that parents do have an important part to play that can be utilized to bring about change.

Clearing up the family mess: working with soiling children

Not all family work needs to be deadly serious at all times and an element of play can be brought in which joins the parents with their problem child through pleasurable activities. Pre-adolescent encopretic children whose symptomatology has no physical causes, and where sexual abuse has been excluded, can be managed by their parents making 'Sneaky Poo' the common enemy who needs to be defeated. The idea behind this approach is to 'externalize' the symptom, in this case soiling (White, 1989). Traditionally parents get increasingly angry with a soiling child and eventually openly blame him or her for 'not trying hard enough'. Instead of assuming that the child deliberately soils him or herself because he or she is angry or upset, the soiling is redefined as an act of oppression by the treacherous character of 'Sneaky Poo' who sneaks up and catches the child unawares, popping out against the child's will. Having reframed the problem in this way, the clinician will try to get everybody's cooperation to become involved in the battle against 'Sneaky Poo' who inhabits the boy or girl's body. All members of the family are encouraged to join forces in order to defeat the common enemy. Enlisting the parents' assistance is crucial for the child to feel supported.

The first step is to ensure that the toilet room, often associated with endless failures, is turned into a comfortable place, possibly decorated with pictures that provide encouragement and strength for the child (Superman, Wonderwoman). About half an hour after each meal the child will 'preventively' visit the toilet for a well-timed short spell (no longer than five minutes). The aim is to expel 'Sneaky Poo' so that he cannot play tricks later on. The child is encouraged to become the boss over the poo and praised when he or she succeeds. The next step is to develop an accident and emergency routine which includes the drawing up of a map depicting the favourite place where 'Sneaky Poo' strikes. The clinician assists the family in then identifying the fastest routes from those places to the toilet. Running practices and time trials are instituted to see whether the child can outrun 'Sneaky Poo'. Over time, child and parents develop strategies to trick him and catch him out (White, 1989).

Carrying out these tasks and rituals brings parents and children together and makes them enjoy mutually supportive and playful interactions. The aim of therapy is to interrupt the vicious cycle connected with the symptoms and to facilitate more functional ones.

Through thick and thin: managing eating disorders

Eating disorders mostly manifest themselves first during adolescence and can often lead to serious chronic disorder later on in life. An approach that focuses on early detection and prevention can be successful in preventing eating disorders from becoming deeply entrenched. To state that the family has a major role to play in maintaining or regulating eating disorders is not to negate that there are many other factors which contribute to *anorexia nervosa* or *bulimia*.

It is mostly adolescent girls who present with symptoms of dieting. It is frequently her mother who first finds out about the girl's eating problems. Mother may try to encourage her daughter to eat more or to eat more healthily, but when this has not brought any tangible results, the family doctor is likely to be consulted.

It is at this crucial juncture that family involvement is important: it is far better than all responsibility for the child's eating and weight being handed over to the doctor. If the doctor becomes the manager, then the parents and the whole family are deprived of managing their eating-disordered member. The family is excluded from the treatment, even though it is now well known that many eating disorders are closely linked with family dynamics (Dare and Szmukler, 1991).

Given that food is very likely to be a highly explosive issue in the family, one can of course understand the parents' wish to 'triangulate' an outsider who may become an object of hate and behind whom the parents can conveniently hide. In fact, they are probably relieved that their daughter is fighting a battle with the doctor rather than with themselves.

At the heart of many an eating disorder is the young person's quest for autonomy which appears to be thwarted by the family, not necessarily for bad reasons. As such families are traditionally very close and conflict-avoidant, it is not possible for the adolescent to fight the usual battles without fearing that the parents might be mortally wounded. Staying out late at night, mixing with unsuitable youngsters, endless arguments and other teenage acts of rebellion usually do not figure in families of anorectics. Food becomes the battleground on which issues of growing up, inter-personal boundaries and separation are fought out. If this battle is prematurely defused by being put into the medical arena, a big opportunity is missed and a repetition of serious episodes of weight loss with massive parental anxiety are more than likely.

Involving the family from the outset means keeping the anxiety inside the family rather than investing it in the family doctor, dietician or child psychiatrist. Working with the family means getting each person's view of what the severity and degree of the eating disorder is. It means establishing what the young person's current weight is and what the young person and parents regard as an acceptable weight. It also means establishing, with all concerned, when and by what means this should be achieved. Tackling all of these issues openly and concretely is very important and is likely to bring out considerable differences, not only between the parents and teenager, but also – though more subtly – between mother and father. For example, it is not uncommon for one parent to state that he would want his daughter's weight to be 'normal' (i.e. 50th percentile) whereas the other parent states that she would be happy if she weighed 'a bit more than now'. While both these views might be correct, as far as the teenager is concerned she is being given two different messages. Which one should she listen to? And what might be the implications of following one parent's advice and not the other's? How can she please both? If she obeys the commands of one parent the other will be disappointed!

It is not uncommon that, when one asks each parent and the teenager what the target weight should be, three different opinions get voiced. Similar disagreements occur when the family discusses ways and timescale of getting the teenager to put on weight. During such exchanges it can be observed how the family turns to the health professional for 'advice' (or arbitration). Discussing the idea of the desired weight might require the health professional to speak about the norm by referring to a standardized height-and-weight chart. However, it should be left up to the parents and young person to come to a mutual agreement and it is precisely this negotiation of 'the treatment' which frequently leads to an opening-up of hitherto hidden conflicts.

The clinician's job is to get the family to decide on targets that everyone can agree to and to get each member to consider how these can be implemented. He or she also has to discuss what the consequences might be if the target were not met. The family might be seen at fortnightly intervals and the clinician monitors what goes on, occasionally raising the family anxiety rather than taking it upon him- or herself to become the agent of change. In this sense therapy goes on after or in between sessions. The family truly manages its patient – and the patient is very likely to challenge the way the family operates. This should be of mutual benefit.

Research shows that parental involvement is by far the most effective way of tackling early-onset eating disorders and family work has the best results in this age group (Dare *et al.*, 1991).

Family crisis work: parasuicidal teenagers

The attempted suicide of a teenager is one of the most serious crises in family life: the 'problem child' is acting-out dangerously. Family intervention at the outset can prove very useful, in terms of both understanding and preventing further suicidal episodes. As many suicidal attempts are a cry for help rather than a genuine wish to end one's life once and for all, it is a unique opportunity for intervention.

Parasuicide is probably the most dramatic communication a young person can make to the family and the world at large. Deciphering the various layers of such a statement can be a complex task and can get lost in the frantic times that surround the acute phase. When a young person is admitted to hospital with acute self-harm, both the medical and the family system are in crisis. This very crisis provides an opportunity for intervention with all participants being open to change, unable to revert to familiar patterns of behaviour in that very unfamiliar situation. Convening the whole family around the hospital bed, with drips and all, has a major impact, as the consequences of dysfunctional communication are all too evident. This dramatic setting intensifies the feelings of despair all round and perhaps uniquely unites the family to find a way forward.

The clinician's task is to get the family to understand what made it impossible for the young person to communicate his or her distress in ways other than engaging in very dangerous behaviour. The following questions, addressed to the parents, aim to elicit reflective answers from everyone concerned:

- 'How do you explain that your child had to go to such extremes to let you know how he or she feels?'
- 'What would have to happen for him or her not to do this again?'
- 'What could you do so that he or she does not have to go to such extremes again?'
- 'How can you help him or her to let you know in less destructive ways?'

These questions are a first attempt to get parents and teenager involved in a dialogue, identifying alternatives. The clinician merely acts as a catalyst, enabling a sustained and focused discussion. There are also some direct questions, aimed at the young person:

- 'What would have to happen for you to be able to say what distresses you without having to go to such extremes?'
- 'How could your parent(s) help you with that?'
- 'How could you let them know that you want their help?'

This type of family meeting will, one hopes, set the stage for further ones, the following day in hospital and a few days later at home. The clinician makes it clear that it is each family member's responsibility to keep that sort of dialogue going, to keep the channels of communication open, so that a further dramatic gesture can be avoided.

This way of proceeding – namely, involving the family primarily in the management of the suicidal teenager – does not exclude individual interviews or sessions with the self-harming teenager. In fact, they are an important part of the assessment process and may also have a useful function in terms of helping teenagers to think about what is and what is not family business. The teenager is a person in his or her own right and this is also made clear by offering parallel family and individual work.

SUMMARY: FROM PROBLEM CHILDREN TO PROBLEM FAMILIES?

Family work almost always usefully complements other treatment approaches. Given that there are usually multiple causes for problem children to present as such, it would be naive to think that family intervention alone is the most effective way of managing problem children. There is, however, a question of sequencing: it would seem that involving the family at the outset is common sense, since it uses the parents and other family members as a resource. If professionals outside the family take on major responsibility too quickly, then the parents above all are deprived of the opportunity to put things right. Otherwise the expert runs the risk of becoming a convenient person on whom the problem child can be dumped, in the almost always unrealistic hope that this expert can sort out the problem child and return him or her 'cured' to the bosom of the family.

The family approach has limitations – some parenting is simply not good enough and unlikely ever to be sufficient. Parents who state that their child has 'always' been a problem, and 'knew' that this child was going to be a problem at the point of birth, are often difficult to manage, as they seem to hang onto some beliefs with almost delusional intensity. Averting such potentially self-fulfilling prophecies can prove extremely difficult and may require serious long-term work with such 'problem parents'. The family approach can sometimes be helpful here, since it aims at connecting current parenting with unresolved issues and beliefs from the past. It frequently turns out that so-called 'problem children' carry a burden on behalf of their families, and freeing the children from this helps not only them, but also their families.

REFERENCES

Asen, K.E. and Tomson, P. (1992) *Family Solutions in Family Practice*. Lancaster: Quay.

Byng-Hall, J. (1985) The family script: a useful bridge between theory and practice. *Journal of Family Therapy*, **7**, 301–5.

Dare, C. and Szmukler, G. (1991) The family therapy of early onset: short history anorexia nervosa. In D.B. Woodside and S. Shekter-Wolfson (eds) *Family Approaches to Eating Disorders*. Washington: American Psychiatric Press.

Minuchin, S. (1974) *Families and Family Therapy*. London: Tavistock.

Palazzoli, M.S., Boscolo, L., Cecchin, G. and Prata, G. (1980) Hypothesizing, circularity, neutrality: three guidelines for the conductor of the session. *Family Process*, **19**, 3–12.

White, M. (1989) Pseudo-encopresis: from avalanche to victory, from vicious to virtuous cycles. In M. White, *Selected Papers*. Adelaide: Dulwich Centre, pp. 115–24.

Name Index

SUBJECT INDEX